"In this refreshing, well-designed curriculum, Gary Smalley comes alongside Christian parents with powerful tools to help their children practically, intentionally, and continually hide the Word in their hearts and minds. What a wonderful resource!"

—REVEREND H. B. LONDON JR., vice president,
church and clergy outreach, Focus on the Family

"As the parents of two little boys, we are vigilant about guarding their hearts! It's priority one in our home, and this brilliant DVD kit by Gary Smalley is just what the doctor ordered. It's firmly grounded and immeasurably practical. In his trademark style, Gary puts the cookies on the bottom shelf with plenty of humor and makes it easy to practice the principles that matter most!"

—DRS. LES AND LESLIE PARROTT, founder, RealRelationships.com;
authors of *The Parent You Want to Be*

ESTABLISH YOUR CHILD'S FAITH THROUGH
SCRIPTURE MEMORY AND MEDITATION

Guarding Your Child's Heart

DR. GARY SMALLEY

NAVPRESS

Discipleship Inside Out™

NavPress is the publishing ministry of The Navigators, an international Christian organization and leader in personal spiritual development. NavPress is committed to helping people grow spiritually and enjoy lives of meaning and hope through personal and group resources that are biblically rooted, culturally relevant, and highly practical.

For a free catalog go to www.NavPress.com
or call 1.800.366.7788 in the United States or 1.800.839.4769 in Canada.

ISBN-13: 978-1-61521-634-5

Cover design by Faceout Studio
Cover images by iStock and Photos.com

Some of the anecdotal illustrations in this book are true to life and are included with the permission of the persons involved. All other illustrations are composites of real situations, and any resemblance to people living or dead is coincidental.

Printed in the United States of America

1 2 3 4 5 6 7 8 / 15 14 13 12 11

Contents

Oct 2, 2011

Introduction

Jesus opened His mouth and spoke the greatest, most wonderful words ever uttered to a crowd on a hillside more than two thousand years ago. He told them that if they would listen carefully to His words, understand them, instill them within their hearts and live them, they would experience the very best, highest quality life possible while living on this earth. Isn't that what we want for ourselves and for our children?

He told them that if they applied His commands, they could ask God for anything and they'd have it. They would gain freedom over every addiction, have God's type of love for others, be greatly blessed, be best friends with God, enjoy peace, patience, joy, kindness, and that they would have enormous self-control that would allow them to take great care of themselves with very low stress. It's an extensive list of Jesus' promises for the abundant life to the people who write His commands upon their hearts. Not one of His commands is burdensome, but all of them give an amazing life to anyone who wants to follow them. Who wouldn't want this promised life (see Matthew 5)?

This promised life is what we all want for our children. In these twelve sessions you'll learn how to teach your children to memorize and meditate on Scripture as a part of their everyday lives. You'll learn about four important commands of Christ and help your kids memorize verses that support these four commands. God's Word will change their thoughts and, therefore, their beliefs. And be assured that this method will change your life too. I've found that these four powerful teachings of Christ are transforming me daily. We're never too old or too young to discover the best life possible — the life Jesus wants us to have.

We'll study in-depth these four wonderful beliefs that Christ wants within your heart and your children's heart:

- Humble yourself (see James 4:6).
- Love God (see Deuteronomy 6:5; Matthew 22:37).

- Love others (see Galatians 5:14).
- Rejoice in trials (see Romans 5:3-5; James 1:2-4).

I'll also briefly mention that the Enemy of God also has four beliefs he's trying to instill within our hearts which, when developed within us, cause most of the destruction on this earth. Most of mankind's evil comes directly from the thoughts that Satan wants branded upon our hearts. Satan came to "steal and kill and destroy" everything that is good within us and our children (John 10:10). And that's what he has done throughout our world. It's time for the followers of Christ to take back our turf from him!

The key to this blessed life is our thoughts and beliefs. Did you know that what you have been *thinking* about every day of your life has produced who you have become as a person? If you worry a lot, have too much stress, are discouraged easily, and exhibit a host of other negative characteristics, you have created beliefs in your heart that are causing these emotions. Most people, myself included, do not realize how extremely powerful their thoughts are. Every thought *will* enter your heart after a few seconds or minutes, and it will reinforce the beliefs that your thoughts have created in your heart during your lifetime.[1]

This truth, for me, has become an amazing life-changing and freeing concept. Today, everything about me is changing toward a much more enriching life in every area. I'm becoming free to enjoy my life like never before. And I've never been happier!

Here's even more amazing truth about how our thoughts build these powerful beliefs within our hearts. Most people have between 20,000 and 60,000 thoughts per day. Each of these thoughts will enter your "heart" after thirty seconds. Each thought will form its own individual chemical and electrical formation during the first few minutes or seconds of unstable time in your brain. Every person will process thoughts at a different rate.

If you are thinking about the words of God, your thoughts will form positive and healing electrical and chemical formations. But, if you are thinking negative thoughts, those negative ones will form toxic and unhealthy formations. I recently read that 87 to 95 percent of all mental and physical sicknesses are caused by a toxic thought life.[2]

If you force yourself to think about Christ's four commandments each day between seven and twelve times, you will start to notice new positive and abundant-life beliefs forming within your heart after only four days. And if you stay focused and alert to your present thoughts and use the power given to you by God to take the negative ones captive while you think of Christ's positive thoughts, you can establish new belief habits of thinking in only twenty-one days.

I'm personally thrilled to take this journey with you, and my deep prayer is for you to experience the same freedom and joy that I am finding. To enjoy God's best with your children is to be blessed beyond imagination. You'll not only be enriched, but you'll discover amazing peace as you watch your kids develop God's solid foundation. Your children will leave your home with the very strength of God and able to face any temptation or trial.

Do You Have a Plan?

Getting Started

Read Ephesians 6:10-13:

> *Finally, be strong in the Lord and in his mighty power. Put on the full armor of God so that you can take your stand against the devil's schemes. For our struggle is not against flesh and blood, but against the rulers, against the authorities, against the powers of this dark world and against the spiritual forces of evil in the heavenly realms. Therefore put on the full armor of God, so that when the day of evil comes, you may be able to stand your ground, and after you have done everything, to stand.*

How does this passage relate to Ephesians 6:1-4?

What are a few of the ways the Enemy has attacked your home?

Broken Promises

How have you prepared your children for the attacks of Satan? Do you have a written plan to protect your children from the attacks of Satan?

Introduction

There is an Enemy who wants to destroy your home. His crosshairs are on your children. He has four very powerful and destructive beliefs that he wants you and your children to hide within your heart. We'll start exploring these four toxic beliefs in the next session. As you look around to what is happening in our world of crime and evil, most of the destruction and negative actions come directly from Satan's four toxic beliefs lodged within mankind's hearts. Since he is the chief liar, he wants to steal your heart away from all that is good, kill everything honorable within you and your children, destroying your marriage, family, and lives (see John 10:10).

But Christ came to bring you and your children abundant, overflowing life. He wants you to have amazing freedom from everything evil and establish within your hearts four powerful beliefs that lead to a blessed life here and eternal life forever.

I can honestly admit to you that I've never been happier in my entire life than I am today. I want to follow all of the 131 teachings of Christ; but to start, I've embraced four of Christ's powerful teachings that alone have enriched me more than I could have ever imagined. I'm even learning how to fit all 131 of Christ's commands into the four that I use every day!

With Satan's clever lying ways, no wonder there is so much crime and destruction in our world today. But, just imagine how many evil and negative thoughts were in the hearts of those who destroyed the World Trade Center? This giant example of evil on September 11, 2001, caught our country off guard. We were not prepared. We did not have the enemy sized up properly. Look at these words from *The 9/11 Commission Report*:

> We learned about an enemy who is sophisticated, patient, disciplined, and lethal. The enemy rallies broad support in the Arab and Muslim world by demanding redress of political grievances, but its hostility

toward us and our values is limitless. Its purpose is to rid the world of religious and political pluralism, the plebiscite, and equal rights for women. It makes no distinction between military and civilian targets. *Collateral damage* is not in its lexicon.

We learned that the institutions charged with protecting our borders, civil aviation, and national security did not understand how grave this threat could be, and did not adjust their policies, plans, and practices to deter or defeat it . . . .

The test before us is to sustain that unity of purpose and meet the challenges now confronting us.

We need to design a balanced strategy for the long haul, to attack terrorists and prevent their ranks from swelling while at the same time protecting our country against future attacks.[1]

This report is the best commentary on Ephesians 6:10-13 that I have ever read:

Finally, be strong in the Lord and in his mighty power. Put on the full armor of God so that you can take your stand against the devil's schemes. For our struggle is not against flesh and blood, but against the rulers, against the authorities, against the powers of this dark world and against the spiritual forces of evil in the heavenly realms. Therefore put on the full armor of God, so that when the day of evil comes, you may be able to stand your ground, and after you have done everything, to stand.

Satan is sophisticated, patient, disciplined, and lethal. He hates your family. He will utilize everything in his arsenal to destroy your marriage and your children. His strategy is to ruin not only your marriage, but also the future marriages of your children.

We must understand how grave this threat really is. We have been given the armor of God to protect our hearts. It is not an accident that Ephesians 6:10-13 follows the Bible's central teaching on marriage and family in Ephesians 5:22 – 6:4. The test before us is to sustain the unity of purpose and meet the challenges now confronting us. We need to design a balanced strategy for the long haul, to put on the full armor of God and prevent Satan from having victory in his future attacks.

Is your home prepared for the attacks of the Enemy? Do you have a plan to guard your child's heart from the impending attacks of Satan?

Parent Point

Every parent needs a deliberate, strategic, and measurable plan to guard his or her child's heart.

Guarding the Parent's Heart

For years you have been imparting thoughts and beliefs to your child's heart that actually come from your own heart. Were you raised in a home with no guarding plan, and now you may be continuing the negative cycle? Here's the great news: You can break any negative, toxic cycle. I did. My father was a very angry man. I made the decision early on in my marriage and family to break the cycle of anger. Why? Because my children get the overflow of my heart. Many of you grew up hearing your parents make statements such as,

- You'd better change your tune pretty quick.
- You act as though the world owes you something.
- You've got a chip on your shoulder.
- You're not going anywhere looking like that.
- I never saw a kid like you.
- Other kids don't try stuff like that.
- I wasn't like that.
- Why can't you be more like your brother/sister?
- I'm your father/mother; as long as you live in my house, you'll do as I say.
- Are you going to apologize to me? Well, "sorry" is just not good enough!
- If I've told you once, I've told you a thousand times.
- We're going to church and when we get there I want you to act like a Christian.

If you've never learned how to guard your own heart, that's where we will start.

Then, just think of how many hours you and your children have been bombarded with the lies of this world through TV, movies, music, magazines, school teachers, friends, and the list goes on and on.

What messages have been written on your heart? Do you know what negative belief is behind them? (You will by the time you finish this entire study.)

*I'm not good enough. I will be alone
I'm not smart enough forever.
No guy wants me.*

Name a few things your parents said to you on a regular basis that were positive.

That I was beautiful er

Name a few things your parents said to you on a regular basis that were negative.

*I don't smile enough
I'm moody*

What statements from your childhood are you repeating to your children?

*How proud I am of them
They are beautiful.*

Red Beliefs Versus Purple Beliefs

Solomon said to "guard your heart, for it is the wellspring of life" (Proverbs 4:23). Your heart is shaped by what you think about all day long. And you alone get to choose what you think about every day.

You can either live in the negative or live in the positive. You can dwell on negative feelings and thoughts of anger, resentment, and get-even tactics. Or you can take the words of the apostle Paul when he said, "Whatever is true, whatever is noble, whatever is right, whatever is pure, whatever is lovely, whatever is admirable—if anything is excellent or praiseworthy—*think* about such things" (Philippians 4:8, emphasis added).

You only have two choices. One, you can think like Christ (as in Philippians 4:8). We will be referring to these as **Red Beliefs** throughout this study. Or, you can think like the prince of the world (negative). We will be referring to these as **Purple Beliefs** throughout this study.

You'll have thousands of thoughts every day whether you like it or not. Which would you rather have? Thoughts controlled by the world and the prince of this world or thoughts controlled by God, filled with love and desire to care for people?

Four Key Beliefs from Scripture

The beliefs of your heart usually come from your parents, or you may pick them up from culture. Thus we are likely to be as happy or unhappy as our parents were or as our culture is as a whole. But I don't want my happiness to be dependent on others, whether it's my parents or the culture in general. I know that God created me to be filled with joy, peace, and love, and therefore, I have been learning to base my beliefs solely on Scripture. It is in Scripture that I have found the four major beliefs I am basing my life on today. These four beliefs will become the foundation for the plan you and your children can develop throughout this study. These are the key beliefs I have been diligent to embed, or hide, in my heart so that they become guiding principles for everything I do in life. And I have found that they work. If we will conform our minds to these four key beliefs that were designed by our Maker, they will put us on top of everything that matters in life.

These four beliefs need to be established firmly in your life so they can in turn be included in your plan and impressed on the hearts of your children. Here is just a brief outline of these four beliefs:

1. **Humble Yourself.** You are promised by Jesus that if you humble yourself before God and think of yourself as a helpless person or as a beggar, unable on your own to create His type of love and power, you will become "poor in Spirit." Then, as this sense of powerlessness grows into a huge belief within your heart, He will give you the kingdom of heaven as a reward today and forever (see Matthew 5:3; James 4:6).

2. **Love God.** If you humble yourself before God and cry out as a beggar for His love and power, He'll reward you so that you in turn can use His love and power to love God with all your heart, soul, mind, and strength (see Deuteronomy 6:5; Matthew 22:37).

3 **Love Others.** If you remain humble before God and cry out as a beggar for His love and power, He'll reward you so that you in turn can use His love and power to love others as you love yourself (see Galatians 5:14).

4. **Rejoice in Trials.** If you remain humble before God and cry out as a beggar for His love and power, He'll reward you so that you in turn can use His love and power to give thanks to Him and even rejoice during *all* circumstances, good and bad (see Romans 5:3-5; James 1:2-4).

I'm seventy years old and more excited about today and what the future brings than at any other time in my life. I live with great hope about today and tomorrow.

What will He inspire me to do today? Help someone I don't even know? Grant forgiveness to someone? Use me to bring others to Him? How will He use me tomorrow? Even the littlest things I do can be used mightily by God. All things are possible through Him (see Matthew 19:26). I get to discover His dreams for me and what He wants to do through me.

Nothing has changed my life more than these four beliefs. As I review and *think on* the Bible verses that support these four beliefs every day, my friends and family are finding that I complain less and serve more. I'm headed for a life of taking no credit. It is the power of God working through my spiritual journey. I find that I am overflowing each day and want to give more and more to Norma, my wife, on her spiritual journey. After all, I cannot give what I do not already have.

The result of embedding these four beliefs in my heart has been almost a complete victory over worry, judging others, irritations, lust, unhealthy eating habits, anger, complaining, disharmony with others, and ingratitude. My stress level is now almost nonexistent. My health is much better than it has been since I was a very young man. My blood pressure is 115/70, and that's after a heart attack. But even if my health fails and chronic aches and pains begin to wrack me, I will still be able to maintain a grateful heart and remain joyful—all because of these beliefs I have implanted in my heart and God's loving power.

Learn these principles and you will reap the wonderful consequences of a much closer walk with God and harmony with others. You'll be thrilled at the growing compassion in your heart toward all people. It all comes as a gift from God when you learn to adjust your deepest beliefs to only a few of the most powerful living words from Scripture. Just think of it, God's Word is Truth (see John 17:17), and you will know this truth, and it will set you free (see John 8:32).

You may be way beyond me in this journey. You may already have these four beliefs firmly hidden in your own heart. If so, that's great. For you, this study may be just a testimony of a person who is excitedly learning to walk with God and take His words and beliefs seriously. If you already know and live by these principles, you will be able to influence your children so that these amazing beliefs can spread throughout the world.

Parent Plan

Acknowledge where you are with a plan for guarding your child's heart:

- We do not have a plan.
- We *have* a plan, but it needs some work.
- We have a solid plan for guarding our child's heart.

Do you believe that Satan has a battle plan for your home? List some ways you've seen the Enemy's plan work in your family.

I'm stupid
not good enough 3 poor self-
esteem

Do not let this catch you off guard. Be prepared with your own plan to guard the hearts of your family.

Memorizing Scripture

In each of these twelve sessions, you'll have Scripture passages for memorization. I will offer a few passages; choose one for your family to memorize. If you're studying one session a week, you have a week to memorize and meditate on that Scripture. You can always take longer if needed. I'm asking you and your family to start with the four Beliefs and find verses that teach them. You might find a number of verses that match. We'll offer some suggested verses at the end of each session. Memorize the ones that light you up the most.

You can customize the verse according to the ages and needs of your children. A younger child may be able to learn one phrase or sentence. An older child can learn a longer passage. Teach them just enough that they can grasp the meaning and meditate on it each day.

Be sure this isn't a forced, negative situation for your kids. Find creative ways to make it fun. Here are some tips about times and ways to help your family memorize:

- While in traffic
- While exercising, running, or walking
- While waiting in lines
- At meals
- While getting ready in the morning
- At bedtime
- By tying the verse to a song or dance
- Sitting in my chair watching TV and memorizing during commercials
- During any boring times I face each week
- Rewarding your children when they finish memorizing

Memorize and Meditate

Above all else, guard your heart, for it is the wellspring of life. (Proverbs 4:23)

I have hidden your word in my heart that I might not sin against you. (Psalm 119:11)

Children, obey your parents in the Lord, for this is right. "Honor your father and mother" — which is the first commandment with a promise — "that it may go well with you and that you may enjoy long life on the earth." Fathers, do not exasperate [create anger in] your children; instead, bring them up in the training and instruction of the Lord. (Ephesians 6:1-4)

Finally, be strong in the Lord and in his mighty power. Put on the full armor of God so that you can take your stand against the devil's schemes. For our struggle is not against flesh and blood, but against the rulers, against the authorities, against the powers of this dark world and against the spiritual forces of evil in the heavenly realms. Therefore put on the full armor of God, so that when the day of evil comes, you may be able to stand your ground, and after you have done everything, to stand. (Ephesians 6:10-13)

How Thoughts Form Your Beliefs

Getting Started

Read Proverbs 4:23:

Above all else, guard your heart, for it is the wellspring of life.

List four observations from this verse.

- Your heart is the most important part of the body.
  Your heart is what bleeds into how you are
- w/ your children

In what ways have you let your heart's guard down?

When wanting something really bad, I would do anything to get it.

What are some of the messages you have been writing on your child's heart?

How much they are loved
Safe environment to talk to their mother.

This would be a good time to pray, rather than go on a guilt trip. This study is to build you up, not tear you down. Ask God to give you practical, solid tools in this session to help you guard your child's heart.

Introduction

I received a precious e-mail from my daughter-in-law that pointed to the power of thoughts and beliefs. I have been helping each of my ten grandchildren understand the importance of memorizing Bible verses and thinking about the words and meaning of each word in the verse several times per day. My daughter-in-law Erin told me about the results of this in her twelve-year-old daughter, Maddy.

> Maddy and Garrison [my son] were picking on each other the other day on the way home from school; (nothing out of the ordinary) but she happened to have made a negative, degrading remark to Garrison in the car and I had sent them to their rooms upon arriving home. So, I took it a step further and told her to give me her cell phone. Well, that wasn't a popular punishment with Maddy, and it took me counting to fourteen before she would hand it to me. But she eventually did! However, what transpired next was the most beautiful thing. She went to her room and I had to leave for a meeting. I asked her older sister, Taylor, to call me if she came sneaking out of her room. On my way home from the meeting, there was a message on my phone so I listened to it. It was Maddy and she was crying softly now and said, "Mom, I'm so sorry . . . I really, really am. I should never have talked to you the way I did. I am so lucky to have you for my mom — I don't even deserve you! And . . . I don't even want my phone back . . . I want you to keep it as long as you think you need to." Of course, I was impressed by this. When I walked in the door there was a letter on the counter. It was the most precious letter I have ever received from one of my kids. She admitted to being wrong and continued to apologize for how she had treated Garrison and me. And how undeserving she was of forgiveness and us as her family. I was blown away!
>
> Later she came in and of course we hugged and talked. I asked her what happened to her. She said she was sitting in her room and remembered what "Grampa" told her about forgiveness and about how you think about a person's positive qualities when you're upset. "Grampa told me that since each of us is commanded to highly honor everyone by using God's love to love and serve others, I realized just how important you are in my life." So, she said she forgave me and then started thinking about what a great mom I was and what a great brother Garrison was. She got it!

I just wanted to say thank you from the bottom of my heart for your influence in not only Maddy's life, but all of my children's lives! Thank you for "walking the walk" and sharing it with us, the grandkids, and the world! It does obviously make a difference . . . even in your own twelve-year-old granddaughter's life!

Love you so much, and I'm full of gratefulness!
Erin

In this session I want to share with you the power of beliefs, where they come from, and what you can do to begin to change any of your own toxic beliefs.

Parent Point

What your children think about all day long establishes their beliefs for life. As a parent, one of your main goals should be helping your children think about the right things.

Guarding the Parent's Heart

Most adults who want to follow God know of at least two or three areas in their lives that sorely need to change. I had a problem with lustful thoughts. You may struggle with the same problem or something altogether different. Perhaps you realize that you are too materialistic. Your lifestyle is too grand, you're caught up in consumerism, and you depend on your possessions for status and security. Using a good concordance, find Scriptures that show you God's view of this subject. You might find Scriptures such as 1 John 2:15: "Do not love the world or anything in the world. If anyone loves the world, the love of the Father is not in him." You can have material things: a house, car, boat, furniture — but don't love them more than loving God. He is life, love, and power to live an abundant life with or without things. All worldly things are nothing more than overflow from knowing and loving Him. If you lose anything you own, you haven't really lost anything of worth compared to your relationship with God.

Or maybe your problem is that you are a consistent complainer. You cannot accept adversity, always thinking your life is less than it should be because you encounter difficulties. You might choose to absorb and chew on Romans 5:3-5: "We also rejoice in our sufferings, because we know that suffering produces perseverance; perseverance, character; and character, hope. And hope does not disappoint us, because God has poured out his love into our hearts by the Holy Spirit, whom he has given us." When these verses become "branded" upon your heart through repeated thoughts on these words and their meaning every day for as few as four days and as long as twenty-one days, you will begin to notice a changed attitude about difficulties and trials.

When God's Word changes you, and your children witness the change, they cannot help but wonder how it came about. "Mom always used to complain every time any little thing went wrong, like the time when she dented the car hurrying home. She moaned and groaned as if the world had come to an end. But look at what just happened: The school just changed the school schedule and messed up her upcoming trip. And I could see God's smile on her face through her pain, and she said, 'The Holy Spirit is pouring a lot of love into my heart because of the disappointment I felt at what happened to me today.' What in the world has come over her?"

When the kids see such a change in you, you can explain to them how it came about. They will see the power of God's Holy Spirit working in your life, and it will impress them enough to try it for themselves. They'll have a *model* to see how it is done when they face whatever character flaws they have in the future.

When the Holy Spirit changes you through the power of His words, as He changed me, you become a living, walking example for others. It's the most effective way to lead people to become more like Christ. It's not what you say, but the evidence of your life modeling God's love that influences the people you love, especially your children.

Like I've said, you have thousands of thoughts each day. When you have a thought, it lingers in your brain for anywhere from thirty seconds to several minutes, and then it seeps into your heart. During those seconds or minutes you can take the negative thoughts captive and deny their entry into your heart. You can do this by "holding the thought" and instantly moving to one or all four of Christ's commands and quoting them out loud or just in your mind. That action blocks the negative, worldly thoughts from entering your heart. That's the secret to this entire study! Thoughts will reach your heart either way, but you have a choice to hide them in your heart or throw them in the trash. You throw an unwanted thought into the trash by lingering on a new thought for thirty seconds or longer. In that amount of time, the first unwanted thought drops to the ground and dies.

What I'm suggesting in this study is for you to memorize Bible verses that you can think on when you have a thought that you don't want entering into your heart and reinforcing an already-established toxic belief.

You can do this all day long if you like, and the more you do it, the faster your toxic beliefs dwindle and become less controlling over your life. Keep doing this process for four days and you'll start to see changes reflecting Christ's attitudes. After twenty-one days, if diligently practiced, this new habit is usually fixed. This action is what I plan to take every day for the rest of my life. It never ends because we will never be just like Christ during our short time on this earth.

All negative thoughts come from the "fear beliefs." And most positive thoughts come from the "love beliefs." This is a major idea, because as these negative thoughts reach your heart, they will look for their negative brothers and sisters. The negative thought will increase the power of those negative beliefs in your heart. Then, you'll keep getting more and more negative thoughts flowing back into your brain. The key is to stop the negatively charged thoughts, hold them in your "hand" and discard them after you have changed them by a new thought from one or all of the four Red Beliefs. You can say to yourself, "There's another one of those negative thoughts trying to sneak in! Oh, no you don't! It's not going to work for you negative suckers anymore! Sorry, I'm shrinking the Purple Beliefs and growing the Red Beliefs. I'll use the new Red Belief: 'Thanking God today for this circumstance because this is the will of God in Christ Jesus!'" (see 1 Thessalonians 5:18).

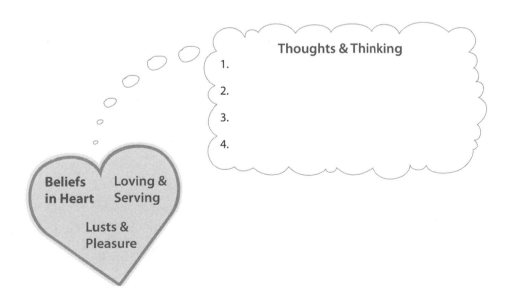

Five Steps to Changing Your Beliefs

Step One: Identify Your Behavior That Needs to Change

My goal for my life—and it is the goal of every follower of Christ—is to be transformed into His image, the kind of person that God intended me to be. And what He intended me to be is quite simple: He created me in His image, which means I am to be like Him, which means I am to be loving, as He is. That means I must change all the motivations within my heart so that most, if not all, of my actions reflect the loving nature of God. So if I'm serious about my commitment to Him, I must do an inventory of my heart, as revealed by my actions, and identify the behaviors that must change. And remember, it's His love and power that enable us to change and do this memorizing and meditating on His words in the first place (see Psalm 51:1-4).

Step Two: Admit the Behaviors in Your Life That Are Not Godly

I think many Christians today are reluctant to admit that their actions are sinful. Even if they realize that certain things they do are not really best, they want to rationalize the behavior or charge it off to some circumstance or event that relieves them of responsibility. When they do this, they rob themselves of this vital second step that will lead to cleansing. I hear many people saying, "Well, everyone else is doing it, it can't be that wrong." I'm reminded each day that it was my sin, along with everyone else's sin, that nailed Christ to the cross.

Step Three: Locate Scripture Verses That Address Your Problem Behavior

The thought of having God cleanse my heart of the contamination of my sins was a wonderful thing. My heart started feeling free and clean. It was exhilarating, and at that moment, I felt extremely grateful to God and closer to Him. But I had to realize that this first cleansing was only a step. The process of transformation in me was not complete. Had I gone on my way, happy to know my heart could be cleaned out, and failed to take the next step, the result would have been disastrous. God had started ridding my heart of one condemnation: lustful thoughts, but it was important that I not leave it cleansed only a small fraction. God started to reduce the Purple Beliefs in my heart, but He still needed to do more within the rest of my life.

Step Four: Memorize Your Selected Scriptures

This is extremely important. You may wonder how latching ont~~~
admonishing us to love God and love others can begin cleansing oui ~~
forming us into His image. Follow my logic here. Common sense says that what
Jesus told us is true: Out of my heart flow my words, thoughts, and actions (see
Luke 6:45). It follows then that since my beliefs live within my heart, as my beliefs
change, so will my words, thoughts, and actions. If I want to be God's servant,
obeying Him naturally, I can embed His words in my heart, and those words will
become my new beliefs. He actually becomes my Boss, my Lord, and my King
automatically when His words form new beliefs in my heart. And as my new beliefs
dictate my behavior, sin begins to vanish little by little from my life because my
behavior conforms to the ideal of God's words.

This logic explains the meaning of Psalm 119:11: "I have hidden your word in
my heart that I might not sin against you." That is why hiding God's Word in my
heart has become so important to me. It is the basis for all the beliefs that will
conform my behavior to the image of God.

Here's another idea to try for you and your children: Try to find a command
of God in any section of the Bible that won't fit into one of the four Red Beliefs. I
haven't been able to find one yet.

Step Five: Deepen the Imprint of God's Words on Your Heart

When I discovered the huge change that came about in my life from hiding God's
Word in my heart, I became like the prophet Jeremiah. He wrote that when he
found God's words, he *ate* them. And he went on to say that those words were his
joy and his heart's delight (see Jeremiah 15:16).

A little after Jeremiah wrote this, he was beaten and imprisoned. He became
discouraged and ready to give up on ministry. He cursed the day he was born and
even cursed the man that came out of the delivery room to announce his birth. But
wait; read on. Jeremiah couldn't give up because God's words flowed through his
veins in such a way that he could not keep from thinking about them. God's words
became part of him—a vital component of his spiritual DNA, ultimately changing everything about his life.

The point is, by meditating, ruminating, chewing, and eating your verses on a
regular basis, you are making them a part of you. You are making God's way of
doing things the *real beliefs of your heart* from which most of your thoughts and
actions will spring.

Parent Plan

Identify the beliefs from the world and clearly communicate them to your children. Let them know that this is *not* what our family is moving toward. We are running in the opposite direction from these four toxic beliefs — the Purple Beliefs! We wish to block the Purple thoughts from now on. (See 1 John 2:15-17 and Galatians 5:19-21 for more about the Purple Beliefs.)

- **Pride** — Jealousy, envy, boasting, judging others, self-centeredness when we don't receive enough recognition and praise for what we have accomplished.
- **Lust of Eyes** — Greed, competition, always wanting more stuff and toys, jealousy, envy, worry, sadness for being without when we don't have enough to make us happy.
- **Lust of Flesh** — Porn, sexual fantasies, the idea that the "good life" is about pleasures, fun, excitement, entertainment, competition, disputes when we don't get our fair share of pleasure.
- **Ungratefulness** — Discouragement, depression, disappointment, hurt, fear, and frustration every time a trial or difficulty hits us.

Identify the beliefs from God that you want to begin imparting to your kids. We want the thoughts and beliefs of Christ in our hearts and minds.

Take a look at the following chart. Sit down with your kids and show them the dichotomy (the contradictory qualities) of these two belief systems. Let them see the areas in your family that need a 180 degree turn.

Fear-Based (Purple)	Love-Based (Red)
Pride	**Humble, Helpless**
Jealousy	Gifted by God: power and love
Envy	Enthused
Self-centered	God- and other-centered
You are your own master	God is your master
You are your own God	God is your God
Lust of Eyes	**Love for God**
Anger: either taking something away or not getting something	Excited anticipation, faith from God, dream big

I'm losing, either way	I'm gaining
Greed, constantly shopping	Desire to give
Competition	Desire to share
I'll smash you so I get mine	I'll lay down my life
Lust of Flesh	**Love for Others**
Sex trafficking	Rescuing kids, adoption
Porn, excess food	Freedom from lust
Sexual immorality, idolatry, selfish ambition	Love, joy, peace, patience, kindness, gentleness
Ungrateful	**Thankfulness**
Discouragement	Freedom from worry and fear
Depression	Treasure hunting for good in pain
Disappointment	Joy from trials
Emotional hurt	Loving our enemies
All types of fear	Cheering difficulties: pom-poms
Frustration	Patience

Imagine that the four worldly, destructive beliefs are a variety of purple rays and the four godly beliefs are various shades of red.

We can decide to block most of the purple-shaded thoughts, which therefore reduces the size and impact of the Purple Beliefs. And the opposite is true. As we block the purple-hued thoughts, our minds can become open to mainly red-colored thoughts, thereby enlarging the four Red Beliefs that can cause those beliefs to dominate our thoughts in our brain.

Another way of seeing this is to imagine the Red Beliefs are lights and the Purple Beliefs are darkness. As a "dark" thought tries to enter our mind, we can "click the light on" by quoting to ourselves one of the Red Scripture verses, and light always drives darkness away.

Is this really possible? An example is New Dad, a former Latino gang leader imprisoned for life after being convicted of murder. Now, he has been paroled out of prison for more than ten years and is married and the father of twins.

We met several times over the years and he kept thinking that, because of his past it would be impossible for him to change and become the man God wanted him to be. I encouraged him to try the "Four-Day Belief Challenge."

"What is that?" he asked.

I explained, "Once you can understand that every thought you have is extremely important and that all of your thoughts reach your heart whether you like it or not, the key is to control which thoughts you allow to enter your heart and which ones you block. You will begin to see major changes in your life after just four days if you are willing to learn this challenge."

He was interested. And in four days almost everything became new for him, including a new job, a new attitude of warmth and loving concern for his wife's feelings, and a deeper love for his precious twins. His wife literally touched his forehead to see if he was delirious. Never have I seen such an amazing miracle in all of my dealings with people over the last fifty years.

The Four-Day Belief Challenge

This "Four-Day Belief Challenge" is generally a summary of this entire study.

Here is a quick summary again. Most people have 20,000 to 60,000 thoughts per day. And in Americans, over half of those thoughts are negative. To help you better understand this process, imagine that every negative and positive thought has its own chemical and electrical makeup. Once they enter the heart of a person, those thoughts will look for their "mother," either the positive or negative "parent beliefs."

One of the most important factors is that all thoughts have a few seconds or minutes delay while they form their electrical and chemical makeup. This is the big secret that can change lives.

Every thought creates or reinforces already created negative or positive *beliefs* in the heart of each person. Our beliefs are the main controllers of our thoughts, words, and actions. *And those three form our emotions.* So the key to a high-quality life is to create beliefs within your heart that control your behavior. We can think whatever thoughts we want, but what would happen if we mainly thought about the words Jesus told us to think about over 2,000 years ago?

This is what this entire study and the Four-Day Belief Challenge is all about: controlling what we think and embracing thoughts that Jesus told us to think, while blocking the thoughts that Satan wants us to think. There are four commands of Jesus that we'll focus on and four opposite worldly beliefs that we encourage you to avoid or block from entering your heart. As we starve and shrink the four worldly beliefs and feed and grow Christ's four commanded beliefs, our lives begin to reflect Christ's nature within four days. And a habit starts forming within twenty-one days.

If you are truly diligent, using God's power to do this challenge, you will start to see changes in your life in just four days or sooner. Diligent effort means you will capture and hold the worldly thoughts for at least thirty seconds, or longer, at one time and think Christ's thoughts during the time you are ignoring the worldly thoughts. As a worldly thought starts to enter your mind, "holding it" means you are ignoring it while you start thinking immediately about the Bible verses that are consistent to what Christ commanded us. For example, take the verse "Blessed are the merciful" (Matthew 5:7). You can think, *Hey, you just offended me!* As a thought like this one starts to enter your mind, ignore it while you think, *I used to get mad easily, God, but now I love being blessed by you because you have given me the power to forgive hurtful people in a hurry.* That's it in a nutshell. Sound easy? It can be after at least one day of practice. Your first day, you should capture at least ten negative worldly thoughts and think only on Christ's thoughts during the capture time. If a former convict can do it, or a ten-year-old grandson can do it, or if someone like me, seventy years old, can do it, I'm sure you can too!

So the Four-Day Belief Challenge is thinking Christ's thoughts that form Christ's beliefs within your heart. It won't take you long to figure out that each Purple thought has an opposite Red Scripture. Think on the Red Scripture and let the Purple ones shrink and die.

King Solomon told us that above everything else you do, guard your heart because out of it flows the wellspring of who you are (see Proverbs 4:23). Since the Word of God tells us that our heart contains our beliefs, let's together start forming the beliefs that honor God.

Here's what the apostle Paul shared with us about beliefs: If a person will agree and admit that Christ is the Boss, or Lord, of his life and, in addition, that person believes that God is real and He sent His Son, Jesus, to die on the cross for our sins and believes that God raised Christ from the grave, that person is saved, meaning rescued, healed (see Romans 10:9-10). For man *believes in his heart*, and the result of believing these things is righteousness. (Righteousness is living in a way where people can see God's love and power in your actions and emotions.)

As a person begins to form the Red Beliefs within his or her heart, that person's actions start to reflect the life of Christ. That's what I long to see parents and their children doing! Thinking the very thoughts that Jesus did and eventually forming His beliefs and acting like Him. This new life is an expression of Psalm 119:11, "I have hidden your word in my heart that I might not sin against you."

That's what you could see in the former gang leader's life and it happened in just four days. This same thing has been happening in my life over the past few years. I've seen major areas of my life transformed after only a few days. I never thought that I would live long enough to understand this awesome and amazing truth from God's Word!

Here is more about the four Christlike beliefs:

1. **Humble yourself**. Christ realized that He only did what He saw His Father doing. He obeyed His Father in all things. He was one with the Father and did as the Father did. He had humbling thoughts by choosing to lay down His life for you and me. He didn't demand to be lifted up in high honor, rather He humbled Himself even to a death on the cross (see Philippians 2:6-8).

   God empowered His Son with His great love and strength. Jesus in turn, empowers us by His Words and His Spirit living within us. Jesus blessed us only after we admitted that we ourselves are humble, poor in spirit, helpless, and unable to create His type of love and power on our own. A humble person is primarily a beggar bowing down and crying out to God for His love, power, and eternal salvation. We must have God's love and power in order to follow the commands of Christ. James said it this way, "God opposes the proud but gives grace to the humble" (4:6). His freely given grace is His power and love enabling us to be motivated to think His thoughts. One of the bigger, more important thoughts He wants us to have is, *Lord, you are my Boss, and I am incapable of doing anything spiritual without you energizing me and giving me your powerful love.* That's humility, and He will greatly bless you (see Matthew 5:3; James 4:6).

2. **Love God**. After humbling ourselves before God, He rewards us with His love and power to enable us to love Him with our entire heart, soul, mind, and strength (see Matthew 22:37). We seek nothing on this earth to be above the value of God and our loving relationship with Him. Everything we get on earth is a gift from God, a mere overflow to knowing and loving Him. We long for Him more than material things; we thirst for Him more than a drink; we hunger for Him more than any food; we crave Him above loving and knowing any other person.

3. **Love others**. As we remain helpless to create God's type of love and power, He rewards us with His grace, enabling us to love Christ, follow His words, and desire to love others by serving them. We catch ourselves wanting to love others. You will see God's actions and emotions in your life after you decide to humble yourself. He is faithful to give you all of Himself, but only to the humble, helpless, poor in spirit, and beggars of His love and power.

4. **Rejoice in trials**. Finally, we keep ourselves thinking humble truths and then start using His love and power to gain the desire and strength to thank Him for anything and everything that we experience on this earth, both good and bad. All things work together for good to those who love God and

are called according to His purpose, which is loving and serving others (see Romans 8:28). Give God thanks for *all* things! He didn't ask us to thank Him only for pleasant things or happy times. No, Jesus told us that if we rejoice in our sufferings, hardships, and difficult times, He would bless us with more of His love and power and more rewards in heaven (see 1 Peter 4:13).

He even told us to boast about our trials because great are our rewards from Him: more patience, more of His character, and more hope. And His hope is never disappointed, because His Holy Spirit will pour into your heart God's amazing love (see Romans 5:5). This one command of Christ has changed me more than any of the other three. My old lifestyle is fading when it comes to complaining, worrying, fretting, blaming others, getting discouraged, feeling depressed, or any of the other negative thoughts and emotions. I block all negative thoughts from entering my heart and only allow praise, thanksgiving, boasting about my trials, cheering my hardships, and basically, giving God thanks for all circumstances for this is God's will in Christ Jesus.

Memorize and Meditate

That if you confess with your mouth, "Jesus is Lord," and believe in your heart that God raised him from the dead, you will be saved. For it is with your heart that you believe and are justified, and it is with your mouth that you confess and are saved. (Romans 10:9-10)

My dear brothers, take note of this: Everyone should be quick to listen, slow to speak and slow to become angry, for man's anger does not bring about the righteous life that God desires. (James 1:19-20)

Finally, brothers, whatever is true, whatever is noble, whatever is right, whatever is pure, whatever is lovely, whatever is admirable — if anything is excellent or praiseworthy — think about such things. (Philippians 4:8)

Above all else, guard your heart, for it is the wellspring of life. (Proverbs 4:23)

Memorize and Meditate

Getting Started

Read Deuteronomy 6:4-9:

> *Hear, O Israel: The LORD our God, the LORD is one. Love the LORD your God with all your heart and with all your soul and with all your strength. These commandments that I give you today are to be upon your hearts. Impress them on your children. Talk about them when you sit at home and when you walk along the road, when you lie down and when you get up. Tie them as symbols on your hands and bind them on your foreheads. Write them on the doorframes of your houses and on your gates.*

What is the main truth we want our children to receive?

They are a blessing from God

How do we get that truth to become part of their lives?

How do we impress God's commandments upon our child's heart?

By living them ourselves.

Introduction

The children of Israel believed in the power of memorizing and meditating on Scripture.

In Deuteronomy 6, Moses refers to three generations of a family:

> These are the commands, decrees and laws the LORD your God directed me to teach you to observe in the land that you are crossing the Jordan to possess, so that you, your children and their children after them may fear the LORD your God as long as you live by keeping all his decrees and commands that I give you, [and then here is the nugget] and so that you may enjoy long life. (verses 1-2)

Fearing God is to stand in awe of Him, lifting Him up as the highest of holies. God is higher in value than anything this world offers us — cars, houses, vacations, sunsets, clothes, makeup, beautiful bodies, and anything else you can think of that you can't live without because life would not be worth living. The fact is, God is the only thing not worth living without!

> Hear, O Israel, and be careful to obey so that it may go well with you and that you may increase greatly in a land flowing with milk and honey, just as the LORD, the God of your fathers, [the previous generations] promised you. Hear, O Israel: The LORD our God, the LORD is one. (verses 3-4)

There is no competition to Him. You are about to possess a land that is full of pagan worship; where other gods are worshipped. He says you must be careful.

Verse 5 says, "Love the LORD your God with all your heart and with all your soul and with all your strength." In Hebrew culture today, verse 6 is the key to all education. This is the verse for every Jew raising their children. It says, "These commandments that I give you today are to be upon your hearts." And this *one* commandment became their *core belief* because they *thought* upon these words every day, all day long. They are to be a part of your life. How do we get this greatest of all commands of God impressed on our children's hearts? What is the best way? Do you teach them in a classroom? Do you have them start writing things down, taking notes, learning how to do all of that? Short answer: No.

Moses gives a different way to teach them in verses 7-9:

Impress them [brand them, place them] on your children. Talk about them [these extremely important words] when you sit at home and when you walk along the road, when you lie down and when you get up. Tie them as symbols on your hands and bind them on your foreheads. Write them on the doorframes of your houses and on your gates.

Everywhere you turn and everywhere you go as a parent, you bring the Lord your God, standing alone with no competition to Him, before your children. That's the key; that's what we want to do for this study. We want to encourage parents on how to impress the teachings of the Lord onto our children. And the absolute two greatest commandments of all are "to love the Lord your God with all your heart and with all your soul and with all your mind and with all your strength. The second is this: 'Love your neighbor as yourself'" (Mark 12:29-31).

The apostle Paul told us that if we just do the second command and love others in the same way that we love ourselves, we are obeying all of the laws and prophets (see Galatians 5:14). One of the main reasons that this is true is because the Greek word *agape* means unconditional love that comes only from God. When we know God and are born of Him, He gives us His love. We can't have *agape* love unless we know God and are born of Him (see 1 John 4:7-8).

John is the same apostle who told us that man *believes* in his heart (see Romans 10:9-10). Your child's heart is influenced by your *words* and your *actions*. There are many ways we like to think kids learn, but it is really our modeling and our influence in our everyday lives that affect our children the most. Howard Hendricks at Dallas Theological Seminary says this, "The church gets children 1 percent of their time in a given week. The school gets children 16 pecent of the time. Mom and Dad and the home get children 83 percent of the time. It's the essence of family life." If I had just one sentence of advice to offer parents, I'd encourage them to drench their minds with Deuteronomy 6:4-9. I really think that is the essence of what family life is all about.

First there is the principle of instruction. You talk about it; you teach it; you correct when necessary. Finally, there is the principle of involvement. You encourage children to apply it in their thinking and their behavior while you are doing it with them.

The key to teaching your children to love God is stated clearly in these verses, Deuteronomy 6:4-9. If you want your children to follow God, you must make God a part of your everyday experiences. You must teach your children to see God in all aspects of life, not just those that are church-related.

This session will teach you the main tool for making the four Red Beliefs part of your child's everyday life.

Parent Point

Memorize Bible verses with your children, and find ways throughout the day to think about (meditate on) the Scriptures.

Guarding the Parent's Heart

Memorize God's Word

> Guard my words as your most precious possession. Write them down, and also keep them deep within your heart. (Proverbs 7:2-3, TLB)

What Jesus told us is obviously true: Out of my heart flow my words, thoughts, and actions. "The good man out of the good treasure of his heart brings forth what is good; and the evil man out of the evil treasure brings forth what is evil; for his mouth speaks from that which fills his heart" (Luke 6:45, NASB).

It follows then that since my beliefs live within my heart, as my beliefs change, so will my words, thoughts, and actions. If I want to be God's servant, obeying Him naturally, I can embed His words in my heart, and those words will become my new beliefs. He actually becomes my Boss, my Lord, and my King automatically when His words form my new beliefs. And as my new beliefs dictate my behavior, sin vanishes little by little from my life because my behavior conforms to the ideal of God's words.

This logic explains the meaning of Psalm 119:11: "I have hidden your word in my heart that I might not sin against you." That is why hiding God's Word in my heart has become so important to me. It is the basis for all the beliefs that will conform my behavior to the image of God.

When I speak of memorizing, I don't mean simply getting the words down so I can recite them by rote like punching a button to play a recording. I mean I chew on these verses, each word one at a time. I chew on the meaning of each word daily until they are not just words in my brain; they are new beliefs deeply branded on my heart. This is so important that I will explain it more fully in the next section.

It's essential to find the meaning of each word in every verse. I live the meanings consciously long before they become part of my natural behavior. I repeat the behavior I know to be right until those behaviors are absorbed into my heart to the point that God's ways become my ways. His ways become normal actions within me, and I no longer have to force myself to act according to His words.

Let's say you and your family are taking a road trip. The kids are antsy and tired of riding. They're picking at each other in the back seat and asking, "Are we there yet?" at the rate of about 2.5 times per mile. Give them a Bible verse to memorize, and as a prize offer to let them choose one activity they love while you are on your trip, whether it's canoeing or rafting, a water park or miniature golf. If such activities don't fit the scope of your trip, let the prize be to stop at the restaurant of the child's choice. As soon as they finish memorizing the verse, they get their choice. Then, the same day, explain in seconds the importance of memorizing a verse. And at least three or four more times that same day, ask them, "Share with us what that verse says again?" Repeating it over and over is the key to long-term memory.

You can offer similar incentives at home. Whoever memorizes this verse first gets to pick the family movie rental for Friday night. And whoever memorizes the most verses by the end of the month gets to spend the day with Mom or Dad at the fun park or something the child has expressed a lot of interest in doing.

Notice that I don't suggest offering money prizes. In fact, notice that all the prizes I mentioned involve relationship—an activity together, a meal together, a movie together, a one-on-one day with a parent. But money is certainly something that I've noticed does turn on most of my grandkids. They've memorized a lot of money from me. I think that my granddaughter Maddy is the best at memorizing for a few bucks. She is so responsible in handling money, and her eyes light up if I say, "Who wants to earn $5 today?" Her hand is up so fast no one can compete.

By being creative and coming up with similar rewards, you accomplish several things at once. You create relationships with your kids, you achieve Scripture memorization, you expose your children to your life and how God works in you, and you make learning God's words a meaningful yet painless and enjoyable activity. When I give money to each of my grandkids, it's always in the context of relating with them. It's always tied to shopping at their favorite store with me or with members of their family. They know ahead of time that we'll spend quite a bit of time going over the meaning of each verse. I like that time the most.

Meditate on God's Word

> [Those who] are always meditating on his laws . . . are like trees along a
> river bank bearing luscious fruit. . . . Their leaves shall never wither, and all
> they do shall prosper. (Psalm 1:2-3, TLB)

Meditation is focused thinking on a verse or section of Scripture in order to form
your beliefs. When I speak of focused thinking, I mean that your *thoughts* are
focused on what Christ or God's followers said in both the New and Old Testaments.
Controlling our thoughts is meditating on Christ's truthful words. Plus, you can
think each word in Christ's commandments and pause long enough to rehearse the
meaning of each word. That's further time spent meditating.

For example, let's say that you start thinking about the decrease in pay you
received from your employer last month. You begin thinking thoughts like, *I actually deserve a raise; I'm working harder than anyone else at the plant. What are they
thinking? I'm really discouraged. I needed that money for our summer vacation. No one
treats their employees like this and then expects the morale to be high. Why don't the
bosses take less and spread it around? I should quit, that would show them what I do
around there!* Notice all of the negative, complaining thinking?

Meditation is breaking in on any one of those negative thoughts and "captur-
ing it." Your aim is to "take captive every thought to make it obedient to Christ"
(2 Corinthians 10:5). Hold on to those negative words while you start thinking
Christ's thoughts. For example, *Lord, I used to complain and gripe about hardships
hitting me or about not making enough money to buy the things we need in our lives,
but no longer. Now, I love and crave you with all of my heart, soul, mind, and strength,
and I cry out to you as a beggar, letting you know what I'm feeling and needing. You're
bigger than my bosses and you can fix this any way you desire. My bosses are not little
gods! I refuse to elevate them to a higher position in my life than they really are. You,
Lord, already know what I need and what my family needs. I can't wait to see how
you'll fix this situation or how you'll use this situation in my life to add more of your
love and power to my life. Plus, I am cheering the pain this is causing me, just waiting
to see all of the gifts you will instill within me because of this situation. And one more
thing, God, HELP ME by providing enough for my family to live and take that vacation. You are more important to me than a vacation, but the vacation gives me more
time to relate and show your love within me to my kids and mate. You've always been
faithful, so I'm here again crying out to you.*

I was just with my good friend Terry Brown, and while we were eating lunch, he told me at least a dozen stories of how God has specifically answered his "crying out prayers" over the past year. God moved people to give him the exact amount for tires, gas for a family trip, and later, I found out about how God gave him exactly enough for a new part he needed to keep his air conditioning going during 100 degree heat. When I left him, I stopped at the eyeglass place to get a bid for replacing my sunglasses I had lost. She told me what the price was and I gasped, "What, why so much?" She told me that prices had almost doubled over the past few weeks. I didn't have peace about spending that much, so I walked out. As I drove home, I prayed, "Lord, you know right where my glasses are; if you find them for me, I'll give the money to Terry." The next morning, my wife held up broken glasses and said, "Are these what you've been looking for?" Yes! I looked at them and decided to fix them. It was easier than I had figured. Later that day, I took the money to Terry and he teared up and said, "That's exactly what that new air conditioning part will cost me!"

Meditation can also happen each time you simply think about any of the four Red Beliefs. I often relax in my bed just before falling to sleep or waking up, I go over as many Bible verses as I can that relate to the four Red Beliefs. I play a game sometimes by just turning to a random page in the Bible and see if I can find a verse that complements one of the four Red Beliefs. I find a lot of them that harmonize with Christ's words.

Parent Plan

Memorizing Scripture helps me:

- **Fight temptation** — "I have hidden your word in my heart that I might not sin against you." (Psalm 119:11)
- **Make good choices** — "Your word is a lamp to my feet and a light for my path." (Psalm 119:105)
- **Live with less stress** — "Your promises to me . . . are my only hope. They give me strength in all my troubles; how they refresh and revive me!" (Psalm 119:49-50, TLB)
- **Be filled with joy** — "Your words are what sustain me . . . . They bring joy to my sorrowing heart and delight me." (Jeremiah 15:16, TLB)

Memorize and Meditate

"Love the Lord your God with all your heart and with all your soul and with all your mind." This is the first and greatest commandment. And the second is like it: "Love your neighbor as yourself." (Matthew 22:37-39)

Blessed is the man
    who does not walk in the counsel of the wicked
or stand in the way of sinners
    or sit in the seat of mockers.
But his delight is in the law of the LORD,
    and on his law he meditates day and night.
He is like a tree planted by streams of water,
    which yields its fruit in season
and whose leaf does not wither.
    Whatever he does prospers.

Not so the wicked!
    They are like chaff
    that the wind blows away.
Therefore the wicked will not stand in the judgment,
    nor sinners in the assembly of the righteous.

For the LORD *watches over the way of the righteous,*
    but the way of the wicked will perish. (Psalm 1, emphasis added)

How can a young man keep his way pure?
    By living according to your word.
I seek you with all my heart;
    do not let me stray from your commands.
I have hidden your word in my heart
    that I might not sin against you. (Psalm 119:9-11)

Four Main Red Belief Verses:

    1. *Blessed are the poor in spirit, for theirs is the kingdom of heaven. (Matthew 5:3)*

    2. *Love the Lord your God with all your heart and with all your soul and with all your mind and with all your strength. (Mark 12:30)*

    3. *"Love your neighbor as yourself." There is no commandment greater than these. (Mark 12:31)*

    4. *Blessed are those who are persecuted because of righteousness, for theirs is the kingdom of heaven. Blessed are you when people insult you, persecute you and falsely say all kinds of evil against you because of me. Rejoice and be glad, because great is your reward in heaven, for in the same way they persecuted the prophets who were before you. (Matthew 5:10-12)*

Belief #1 — Humble Yourself

Getting Started

Read James 4:6 and Matthew 5:3:

> *God opposes the proud but gives grace to the humble. (James 4:6)*

> *Blessed are the poor in spirit, for theirs is the kingdom of heaven. (Matthew 5:3)*

How do these two verses go together?

How does God oppose the proud?

What does it mean to be humble, or poor in spirit?

Introduction

We want our kids to be successful. We want them to be winners. We don't like the idea of surrendering because it seems like the opposite of winning. It looks to us like loss or weakness. When we surrender we wave the white flag and concede that the fight is over. In World War II, Japan and Germany surrendered when they realized that America and its allies were stronger than they were, and to continue the fight could mean total annihilation.

But when you surrender to God, the opposite happens. You don't lose; you win. You become strong. When you give up and surrender, you find your life instead of losing it.

This is a wonderful paradox we find when we come to God. He is always fresh and surprising. In the spiritual world, if you want to gain your life, you must lose it. If you want to be first, you must position yourself to be last (see Mark 9:35). If you want to be rich with life, love, and power, you must become poor in spirit (an attitude of being humble, helpless, a beggar toward God).

On Sundays our pastor loves to say, "Grab a cup of Starbucks in our coffee shop, find a seat, then die." It sounds shocking, but dying to all of your selfish desires is the only way to live. The only true way we can find the fulfillment Jesus offers in the Christian life is to die daily to ourselves and accept the real life He offers. The cross of Christ is the symbol of death. So, when we "take up our cross daily and follow [Christ]," we are actually dying to being the boss of our own life and submitting to Christ's will of loving God and others and watching God build His love and power within us so that we can live out Christ's will (see Luke 9:22-26).

That's what it means to surrender. In other words, you die to life as you want it, or as the world advises you to live, and live only by what God says in His Word. He designed us, and He wrote the instruction manual. When you and I brand His words upon our hearts, we begin to enjoy the life God designed us to have.

The bottom line (and I will mention this over and over so that it sticks in your mind) is this: His highest will for us is twofold—to love and crave to have Him and to love and crave to serve others. That's it. To surrender to these two commands is to find life at its best. The apostle Paul said it this way: "The entire law is summed up in a single command: 'Love your neighbor as yourself'" (Galatians 5:14). Life becomes so much simpler when we realize that this one thing pleases God and that we're loving Him when we love others.

When we surrender to God, we give up trying to figure out the best and most fruitful ways of living our lives. When we surrender we give up and admit that our own way has gotten us into a deep rut, or even into addictions, misery, unhappiness, bitterness, or a destructive lifestyle. When we go our own way we are fighting against God, for He designed us to function with Him in the driver's seat. Just today I realized that if I continue to sit on the "throne of my life" and demand to be in charge of my life, God resists me and I lose the opportunity to have His type of love and power. I don't ever want to lose God's love within me!

All I'm really describing here is the word "sin." *Sin* is doing life your way and ignoring God's ways. When you're the driver, the boss, the king of your own life, you are in sin, plain and simple. So when we surrender, we stop fighting against God. We realize He is more powerful, and He has us pinned to the mat. The greatest part of doing His will is that He not only gives us His love when we admit our weakness but we also get to use His love to love Him and others. To me, that's a no-brainer.

Parent Point

Teach your child that humility is the secret to being filled by God. Can we actually tell people that we are humble? Yes, as long as we understand that *humble* means "helplessness, powerlessness."

Guarding the Parent's Heart

Just imagine? As we remain humble, we gain the very power within ourselves that God used to raise Christ from the grave. What could we do with this unlimited power? Wow! Let that sink in for a few moments.

The first step is to reflect on the meaning of each word or key phrase in Matthew 5:3. The first word I focus on is *blessed*. The dictionary uses some great words to define the word *blessed* such as "sacred, holy, supremely favored, and fortunate." Part of the word *blessing* means, "I am highly honored by God." Isn't that amazing?! I'm highly valued by God above all of His material creations. I am supremely favored. I am endowed with His many blessings He wants me to enjoy. I am fulfilled, happy, and complete in Him. Talk about being truly blessed!

Next, I think about the meaning of *poor in spirit*. There are three basic meanings of those words.

The first one is that you are being humble, a beggar, helpless, or aware that you are like a newborn baby. You are being humble (poor in spirit) when you admit that you don't have any hint of God's love or power within your natural self. You are nothing more than a beggar crying out to a holy God for His love and power. Like a beggar, a really poor person has nothing. So I say to God, "I don't have any power, character, or love like you have. I'm human with no capacity to manufacture your type of love or power." Then I go through a series of thoughts about what being a *beggar* means. I am helpless, shipwrecked, or bankrupt. I see myself with my face in the dust as a spiritual beggar. I cry out to God, "Please give me your grace, your love and power through both your Holy Spirit and the power of your living words living within me" (see Hebrews 4:12). "When I know your words, God, which is Truth, your Truth sets me free" (see John 8:31-32). The love that God gives is unlimited caring for others more than I care for myself. Often I go to 1 Corinthians 13 and repeat back to God, with thanksgiving, all of the qualities of love that I don't have on my own. (Love is patient, kind, humble, selfless, and so on.) Then, I tell God that I can't wait for Him to build these love qualities into my life because I remain "poor in spirit." To those who are humble, God gives all the tools and abilities to become like Him (see 1 Peter 5:5).

Consider the powerful idea of Jesus as the True Vine (John 15:1-8). We are helpless unless God grafts us onto His Vine, Jesus Christ. If grapes symbolize God's love and power, we are like twigs unable to produce fruit with our own efforts. God nurtures us through His Holy Spirit and through His powerful, living Word (see Hebrews 4:12). Christ's words are like powerful sap flowing into us as twigs. After a while, you will begin to see the fruit of the Spirit start to grow on and within you. At first, you'll start seeing His power, love, joy, peace, and so on, as only small green flower buds reflected in your behavior. But in time, each bud will continue to grow until it becomes a fully ripened red grape, delicious to the taste of all who are in contact with you. You will become the sweet, loving taste of Christ, but only if you remain a helpless twig, like a beggar. If you try to push the grapes out early with your own efforts, you can destroy them in your life. If you could produce your own grapes, you would most likely become boastful or prideful.

Poor in spirit can also mean to "low list" yourself under the people you happen to be with at any given time. It means to put yourself last after other people in your life. You will be more concerned about others' well-being before yourself. You may not feel any different, but others will see your actions eventually. As an "abider," you aren't trying to "massage" the buds to turn them into grapes. God gives you the fruit of the Spirit without any effort on your part. It's a gift of love to you. That's what God's grace is, a gift of His love and power to only the helpless (see Ephesians 2:8-9). You'll catch yourself loving others with a new power and desire to love. Those who wait upon the Lord will find themselves, in time, soaring like eagles (see Isaiah 40:31).

The third meaning of *poor in spirit* is having an awareness that you are spiritually dead. Galatians 2:20 says, "I have been crucified with Christ and I no longer live, but Christ lives in me. The life I live in the body, I live by faith in the Son of God, who loved me and gave himself for me." When I meditate on that verse, I recognize that I am helpless, a beggar, and that there is no one more helpless than someone who is dead, hanging onto an imaginary cross. God is now my new Boss, my Lord, my Master. One of the major reflections of being prideful is maintaining the ownership of your life. "No one will be telling me what to do. I will do as I want, when I want." As I humble myself before God, I remind myself many times during a typical day that I just want to do His will, which is never a burden. His yoke is light. He desires for me to remain helpless and a beggar for His best for me: His love and power and overflowing Spirit filling me up to all of the fullness of Himself! He wants me to believe what He believes — the Red Beliefs.

So, as I'm meditating, I tell God that I am indeed crucified with Christ. (Gary Smalley doesn't live for just himself anymore; he is voluntarily hanging on the cross with Christ.) Then I say, "But I'm still alive." Now I live by the faith of the Son of God. What is Christ's faith? Loving God with all my heart, soul, mind, and strength, and loving others as myself. His vision is the kingdom of God on earth. To love God and others and keep living in His power each day is His bottom-line will for all of us. But, again, He only gives His love and power to the spiritually helpless (see James 4:6).

Here is my Galatians 2:20 "Living Death Certificate." It hangs on my office wall.

Here lies Gary T. Smalley
Born September 18, 1940
Died to Self June 18, 1968
He now lives his life for Christ and from the power and love of Christ

Parent Plan

Make a list of all the ways pride and humility are displayed in your home.

Can you identify the beliefs in this list—Purple or Red?

Next to each belief listed above, write the opposite belief (Purple versus Red).

The key will be to go over the Red Beliefs each day before you leave the house.

I finally understand that daily is the key to success in staying humble. You must chew on God's words daily in order to embed them into your heart. Several sections of Scripture warn us about neglecting His words and not having a daily habit of reviewing them. Oh, how easy it is to allow the weeds, cares, and lack of watering and nurturing to choke out God's words from our hearts. When this happens, the world's beliefs and our natural flesh take over our lives quickly. Remain humble by emptying yourself each morning before you jump out of bed and your feet hit the floor. Remind your children before you send them out of the house each day.

Memorize and Meditate

God opposes the proud but gives grace to the humble. (James 4:6)

Blessed are the poor in spirit, for theirs is the kingdom of heaven. (Matthew 5:3)

I pray that out of his glorious riches he may strengthen you with power through his Spirit in your inner being, so that Christ may dwell in your hearts through faith. And I pray that you, being rooted and established in love, may have power, together with all the saints, to grasp how wide and long and high and deep is the love of Christ, and to know this love that surpasses knowledge — that you may be filled to the measure of all the fullness of God. Now to him who is able to do immeasurably more than all we ask or imagine, according to his power that is at work within us. (Ephesians 3:16-20)

For it is by grace you have been saved, through faith — and this not from yourselves, it is the gift of God — not by works, so that no one can boast. (Ephesians 2:8-9)

And what does the LORD require of you? To act justly and to love mercy and to walk humbly with your God. (Micah 6:8)

Practicing Humility in the Family

Getting Started

Read Matthew 6:12:

Forgive us our debts, as we also have forgiven our debtors.

What is the practical application of humility in this verse?

First, whom do you need to forgive in your life?

Second, whom do you need to seek forgiveness from?

Introduction

Christ realized that He only did what He saw His Father doing. He obeyed His Father in all things. He was one with the Father and did as the Father did. He had humbling thoughts by choosing to lay down His life for you and me. He didn't demand to be lifted up in high honor, rather He humbled Himself even to a death on the cross (see Philippians 2:6-8).

God the Father, empowered His Son with His great love and strength. Jesus in turn, empowers us by His Word and His Spirit living within us.

The reason I'm constantly giving you extremely important reminders throughout this study is that Jesus blessed us only after we admitted that we ourselves are humble, poor in spirit, helpless, and unable to create His type of love and power on our own. I'm rehashing these simple but powerful truths because the more you read them and the deeper you understand them and think about them, the larger the Red Beliefs will grow within your heart. Daily repetition is so important, as Moses showed us in Deuteronomy 6:4-9.

A humble person is primarily a beggar, bowing down and crying out to God for His love, power, and eternal salvation. It took me several months before it finally sank into my heart that I must have God's love and power in order to follow the commands of Christ. Again, James 4:6 said it this way: "God opposes the proud but gives grace to the humble." His freely given grace is His power and love, enabling us to be motivated to think His thoughts. One of the bigger, more important thoughts He wants us to have is, *Lord, you are my Boss, and I am incapable of doing anything spiritual without you energizing me and giving me your powerful love.* That's humility, and He will greatly bless you (see Matthew 5:3 and James 4:6). Only those who abide in His words, who follow His commands, are His true disciples (see John 8:31-32).

Do you see how valuable you are to God? How is your self-confidence after realizing that God is your confidence? Do you believe in yourself? Are you humble? Is there any pride or arrogance in your life? There is a fine line between having self-confidence and not being prideful. Many of us never seem to be able to find this line. As I think back over my own life, I can clearly remember being so helpless while I lived in Waco, Texas. We had three children, and our finances were tight. I was making about $15,000 per year after taxes. But that didn't bother anyone in my family because we were all learning how to depend upon God. My daughter, Kari, and I were crying out to God each night, over a year, for a different car because our car was falling apart little by little, and I knew it had about two months left. One day, a friend of mine was visiting our home and suggested that we go to lunch. "Let me drive," my friend said, and he drove my car. As we headed for the restaurant, he was sinking in the seat because the springs were broken. We were very good friends and he felt free to comment, "This is pathetic. Who drives a car like this?" I laughed with him. Then he said, "Tomorrow, after our meeting, I want you to go to any car lot and buy yourself a new car." That was the only time God has ever given us a car and the only time I've ever prayed for one. Kari and I were humbled and blessed by God that day.

After remaining helpless to earn extra money for my family, I continued to cry out to God to enlarge my influence with marriages and families all over the world. When God opened so many doors for me to minister to marriages everywhere, I started making more money, and within ten years, little by little, pride crept into my heart. I could feel God leaving me during that time. I didn't know what was wrong, but after a heart attack and kidney transplant, God showed me that I had been managing His financial rewards, and I had walked away from the Rewarder. I had become my own boss. I started believing that *I* was the one helping all of these couples around the world. I became all of the characteristics of a proud person.

After the kidney transplant, God got my attention, and I started all over again learning how to humble myself before Him. He began to rekindle my heart with His words, and now I'm back with Him 100 percent. He is my life, my joy, my freedom, and my healing.

I find that it's hard to find the right sweet spot in having a good self-value and yet not having arrogance or pride in my life. My new value comes because He loves me. There should be no pride or arrogance operating in our lives. However, we should have self-confidence. The difference, I believe, is that confidence comes when we know that God is the reason we are able to do what we do. He is the one who gave us our gifts and talents. Confidence comes from God, and pride comes from us and the prince of this world.

Pastor John Piper puts it this way:

"God opposes the proud, but gives grace to the humble" (1 Peter 5:5), and "Everyone who exalts himself will be humbled, and he who humbles himself will be exalted" (Luke 14:11). God has told us at least five things about humility.

1. Humility begins with a sense of subordination to God in Christ. "A disciple is not above his teacher, nor a slave above his master" (*Matthew 10:24*). "Humble yourselves under the mighty hand of God" (*1 Peter 5:6*).

2. Humility does not feel a right to better treatment than Jesus got. "If they have called the head of the house Beelzebub, how much more will they malign the members of his household!" (*Matthew 10:25*). Therefore humility does not return evil for evil. It is not life based on its perceived rights. "Christ also suffered for you, leaving you an example for you to follow in His steps . . . . While suffering, He uttered no threats, but handed [his cause] over to Him who judges righteously" (*1 Peter 2:21-23*).

3. Humility asserts truth not to bolster ego with control or with triumphs in debate, but as service to Christ and love to the adversary. "Love rejoices in the truth" (*1 Corinthians 13:6*). "What I [Jesus] tell you in the darkness, speak in the light . . . . Do not fear" (*Matthew 10:27-28*). "We do not preach ourselves but Christ Jesus as Lord, and ourselves as your bond-servants for Jesus' sake" (*2 Corinthians 4:5*).

4. Humility knows it is dependent on grace for all knowing and believing. "What do you have that you did not receive? And if you did receive it, why do you boast as if you had not received it?" (*1 Corinthians 4:7*). "In humility receive the word implanted, which is able to save your souls" (*James 1:21*).

5. Humility knows it is fallible, and so considers criticism and learns from it; but also knows that God has made provision for human conviction and that he calls us to persuade others. "We see in a mirror dimly, but then face to face; now I know in part, but then I will know fully just as I also have been fully known" (*1 Corinthians 13:12*). "A wise man is he who listens to counsel" (*Proverbs 12:15*). "Therefore, knowing the fear of the Lord, we persuade men" (*2 Corinthians 5:11*).[1]

Crying out to God each day as a helpless beggar is the only way we can truly experience life to the fullest. My prayer is that by the end of this session you will be crying out to God for His power and love.

Parent Point

Keep anger low and honor high in the home by seeking forgiveness.

Guarding the Parent's Heart

Pride means being the boss of your own life. You decide when and where to live your life. You choose to become your own little god. You create, you plan, you build the life you want. Look at what happens in the world when humans take control. Look around at the countries, including America, that are so evil, greedy, addicted, perverted, miserable, warring, and so many other negative things.

When we follow Satan's plan, we are boastful, proud, and braggy. We elevate people to the position of little gods, which leads to fear, worry, anxiety, and a critical attitude. We sometimes give people way too much power over us because we blame them for making us miserable. Is God too small to overcome all that we face as humans? Can God not fix our messes we get ourselves into? Can people override God's will for us? The apostle Paul made the point that we can take no credit for anything since everything good comes from God (see 2 Corinthians 3:4-5). That understanding leaves no room for boasting about what we have accomplished.

Isn't it interesting how much power we give to ourselves and to Satan's world to control us? If we think like the world thinks, then we will have the Purple Beliefs of the world and all of its miserable consequences. But if we think like Christ did, we will have His beliefs—the Red Beliefs—and get the consequences of them: love, peace, joy, patience, kindness, goodness, faithfulness, and self-control. Which consequences do you want for yourself as parents and for your children?

God gives His grace to the humble, the helpless, the ones who know that they cannot manage life without Him. They can't create the same kind of love and power that God gives. So, the humble beg God day and night for His wonderful qualities given only to the beggars.

I once worked for a very large Christian ministry, and over time I grew to dislike and distrust the leaders. I blamed them for my unhappiness, and when I finally quit, I thought that they had taken my past and wasted it. I thought they had ruined my life and set me back years from making a decent living. I felt like I had to start all over again because of the wasted years; somewhat the way many divorced people reason. But, my thinking was very wrong and toxic.

When I finally realized that God is my loving Master, guiding me into an overflowing life of love and power, I relaxed and turned my life over to him 100 percent. I rested in Him because He is more loving and powerful than my old bosses. I didn't waste any time. What did I think that I had lost? Money and a better vocation? No, I won the secret to gaining what most people desire anyway: peace that brings the highest quality of life with God. And when we humble ourselves before Him and trust in Him as our only source of a high-quality life, then we gain the life He promised us, because He only gives it to the humble. I was miserable and hurting for a while, but out of that experience came a better understanding of what people feel after divorce and what many husbands and wives feel in an angry marriage. For everything that God called me to do in the late 70s, 80s, and 90s, God used my memory of pain and the joy of knowing that God blesses those who suffer with more of His refining love. I wouldn't take back that pain I went through for anything.

What helps us continue walking in humility?

Thinking humble thoughts all day long by admitting and holding proud thoughts while we meditate on Bible verses that we have memorized about staying humble. For example, "Lord, thank you so much for blessing me as I remain aware of how poor I am at doing anything worthwhile on my own spiritually."

Realizing that every cell in my body was created by God and I can't do anything by myself. I thank God all of the time for making me and giving me my brain, body, personality, and abilities. He gave me the raw stuff and then He empowered me to use what He created to do the many things that I have done, but none of them would have been possible without Him in the first place.

Parent Plan

Forgiving and seeking forgiveness from our children and other loved ones is an important way to show humility. Admitting when we have offended someone is always humbling. I offended my family members many times over the years, and each time I recognized their emotional pain, I would swallow hard and approach the offended person with sadness that he or she had to put up with someone like me who was often blind to my insensitive actions or words.

When seeking forgiveness, you may want to keep three things in mind:

First, remember that your approach sets the tone of the conversation. Your voice should be soft and receptive to the other person's feelings and attitude.

Everything needs to be soft, from tender touch to the sincerity in our voice.

I like to ask myself, "How helpless am I right now? How willing am I to hear what the offended person might say?" If I have rehearsed my rebuttal, I'm probably not ready. Too many times we want to blame others for the hurt *we* cause. Blaming only invalidates our loved ones.

Second, ask specifically how you hurt your loved one. Often we can be wrong about what we did to hurt the person we love. This is a major step toward validating their feelings and needs when we ask them how they were hurt by our words or actions.

This allows the person we love to share their feelings, and if they don't want to share them at the moment, then take time to let them build their thoughts. Or, you can even ask questions that might help your loved one understand more clearly how you hurt him or her.

Third, worry only about your own faults. Don't consume your energy on worrying about what your loved ones did to you. We are not in control of them, and thus we can't make them seek forgiveness nor accept our own forgiveness. We can only control our own lives and how we behave toward our loved ones.

I have heard parents scold their children and demand that they seek forgiveness from another member of the family or a friend. When a parent forces repentance, it can teach a child that genuine feelings don't really matter. I remember helping my son Greg seek his brother Michael's forgiveness once when I caught him sitting on Michael and performing the "Alaskan Torture." He was thumping Michael on the chest with his knuckles until it was turning red like an Alaskan volcano. I walked out to the front yard when I heard Michael screaming.

I called out, "Greg, get off of him; what are you doing?"

"Nothing," he responded.

"Nothing? Then why is his chest so red?"

"I was teaching him about the Alaskan tradition," he said sheepishly.

"It looked more like you were torturing him," I said.

He replied, "No, every kids needs to learn this old tradition."

I led him into the house and sat him down in the living room. I said, "Greg, do you remember when we lived in Waco and those kids down the street jumped you and tied you to that tree?"

His head nodded, yes, with embarrassment.

"When I chased them away and told their parents what had happened, do you remember what their parents did to their own children?"

"Yes, they all came down and asked for my forgiveness, and the next day, we started playing together again."

"How did that make you feel, being tied up?"

"Terrible!"

"Do you think Michael feels the same way right now that you did back then?"

"Yes, probably," he answered.

"I'll let you figure out what you might want to do."

It wasn't ten minutes until I witnessed Greg seeking Michael's forgiveness. Most of the time, if you wait until your children understand and feel the pain they inflicted on a sibling or relative or friend, they'll more willingly try to correct the offense.

By humbly seeking forgiveness, acknowledging every aspect of wrongdoing on your part, you are cleaning up your end. God does not hold us responsible for another's sin—only our own—so by cleaning up your end you are wiping your slate clean.

Four Actions to Help Guard Your Child's Heart

1. Practice High Honor

Honor is, first and foremost, a decision. It is the simple decision to place high value, worth, and importance on another person, to view him or her as a priceless gift and grant that person a position in your life worthy of great respect. "For where your treasure is, there your heart will be also" (Matthew 6:21, NASB).

Love involves putting that decision into action. In other words, honor is a gift we give to others. It isn't purchased by their actions or contingent on our emotions. You're giving them distinction whether or not they like it, want it, or deserve it. It's a *conferring distinction*, much like an honorary degree. You give honor to a loved one merely because that person is alive and breathing, not because he or she has done something to deserve it. You just do it; it's a decision *you* make. You will soon see honoring your children or mate gives legs to the words "I love you." It puts that statement into action.

Honor is not only the first step of love, it's also the single most important principle for building an intimate relationship. The definition of *honor* is "to give preference to someone by attaching high value to them." When you confer honor you're thinking, *I'm married to an extremely valuable person* or *Each of my children is highly valuable to me.* I'm making the decision to consider him or her even more important than I consider myself to be. Honor is the goal, the prize, the hope that you bestow upon your mate. No one ever reaches perfection, but that hope is always before you; it both guides your relationship and regulates it. I've found that honor can be a reminder; it makes me want to repair any damage I cause in my relationship, simply because I honor my mate.

Jesus told us that whatever a man treasures, that's where his heart will be also (see Luke 12:34). Our affection and love for someone always follows how valuable that person is to us. I usually tell myself that God's value is a "10" to me (1=low value and 10=the highest value). My wife is a "9" and my children and grandchildren are all "8." Those numbers can change depending upon what they do to me, but I keep pushing the numbers back up to their original value to me.

2. KEEP ANGER LOW

Anger is an emotion. Like all of our emotions, there's nothing wrong with it, in and of itself. It's our human response to something that occurs, or at least to our perception of that occurrence. In fact, some anger is good; we get angry when we see an injustice or when someone is trying to violate our personal property lines. In such cases, our anger is what motivates us to take appropriate action. But after anger motivates us to do something good, we can't afford to let it linger inside us. We have to get it out. Anger is a good emotion when it gets us moving, but if we let it take root, we set ourselves up for a great deal of potential harm.

Dr. Howard Markman of Denver University, a leading expert in relationships, gives a strong warning about hidden anger. He reminds us that all those little discussions that just don't seem to get resolved and continually provoke an inappropriate outburst—issues that don't necessarily amount to much, such as whether the toilet seat is up or down—are usually driven by anger that's just below the surface. No matter how many times you try to resolve those issues or enter into deeper intimacy, the anger can keep you in turmoil. Living with angry people is like living in a minefield. If you say or do the wrong thing, *kaboom!* They explode all over everyone. And you're left thinking, *Oh, I had no idea that one thing I did would cause such a reaction.*

Actually, anger is a secondary emotion, not a primary feeling. It arises out of *fear, frustration, hurt,* or some combination of these three. For example, if someone says something harsh to us we first feel hurt and then anger. When we strip the word *anger* down to its deepest level, we see the thread of unfulfilled expectations. *Frustration* is not receiving what we had expected from other people or from circumstances.

Immediately go to God when you get frustrated or hurt. Replace your anger with more of Him.

3. Seek Forgiveness

Forgiveness involves pardon. Basically, that is like erasing their offenses toward us from a marking board. We immediately wash their offenses away like a wave washing away a message in the sand. Second, forgiveness involves caring for the offending person because most people who offend us have something in their own heart that needs healing. When we forgive others, they are released from our anger and we are healed by God. If you remember the Lord's Prayer, one of the petitions is, "Forgive us our sins [trespasses], as we have forgiven those who sin [trespass] against us" (NLT). It suggests that if we forgive others (pardon and help release them), then our Father in heaven will forgive us (pardon and release us). Forgiveness helps the offended person as much as the one who offends. Taking personal responsibility means accepting our part of the offense and seeking forgiveness for where we are wrong. That completes the dynamic in this part of the Lord's Prayer. Remember, if you don't forgive, it's like taking poison and waiting for the other person to get sick.

Prolonged and unforgiven anger is a form of pride. And since God resists the proud, He will resist the unforgiving angry person because that angry person is really shaking his fists in God's face, calling God a liar. It's God's words that tell us that He will work all things happening to us together for our good if we love Him and love others (see Romans 8:28). But if we remain angry past the sun going down (see Ephesians 4:26), we are calling God a liar because we don't believe that God can work something that has happened to us for our good.

4. Find Ways to Serve Each Other

Here are some practical ways you can begin serving the members of your family today:

- My family needs to feel valued—more valuable to me than my job, my friends, or my hobbies.
- My family needs open and unobstructed communication. If this has not been your habit, then work on it a little at a time.
- My family needs my shoulder before my mouth. Empathy and comfort should precede advice or a solution to the problem.
- My family needs to be held and touched. God made us to connect, and meaningful touch is incredibly powerful.
- My family needs to be praised verbally. Praise shows that you notice and appreciate what they do. The lack of praise conveys little worth.

- My family needs help. The best help is without commentary on the way the other does things. If you are unsure how to help, ask for direction.
- My family needs the basics: food, water, shelter, warmth, touch, validation by listening and understanding.

Memorize and Meditate

In your anger do not sin: Do not let the sun go down while you are still angry, and do not give the devil a foothold. (Ephesians 4:26-27)

Forgive us our debts, as we also have forgiven our debtors. (Matthew 6:12)

If we confess our sins, he is faithful and just and will forgive us our sins and purify us from all unrighteousness. (1 John 1:9)

Therefore, if you are offering your gift at the altar and there remember that your brother has something against you, leave your gift there in front of the altar. First go and be reconciled to your brother; then come and offer your gift. (Matthew 5:23-24)

Additional Bible Reading on Humility:
Matthew 18:2-4
Matthew 20:25-28
Matthew 23:1-8
Luke 14:8-11
Luke 18:9-14
John 13:12-17

Belief #2 — Love God

Getting Started

Read 1 John 4:7-8:

> *Dear friends, let us love one another, for love comes from God. Everyone who loves has been born of God and knows God. Whoever does not love does not know God, because God is love.*

Can we, in our own abilities, love God with our whole heart, soul, mind, and strength?

Who is the source of love?

When we are unable to love others, what does it say about our relationship to God?

What do we have to do toward God before He gives us His amazing love?

Introduction

Every day, Mom and Dad, you are painting a picture of God for your children.

As much as we would like to think our children's image of God comes straight from the Bible and the teachings of the church, we sometimes project onto God the unloving characteristics of the people who most strongly influence us. For example, one of the often used biblical terms for God is *Father*. God is referred to as *Father* 187 times in the four Gospels. What does that term call to your mind?

For some fortunate people the idea of God as Father presents a comforting, loving, and protective image that accurately reflects the nature of the true God. But this is not the case for many others. Imagine a little girl of seven who has known only rejection and abuse from her father. What will be her perception of God when her Sunday school teacher tells her that God is like a Father? She will likely see God as an unstable, rejecting, abusing person she cannot trust. The term *Father* may cause others to see God as distant, impersonal, and uncaring, or like a drill sergeant, demanding and angry, with no tolerance for mistakes. Those who were not blessed with good fathers will need to see past their bad experiences and understand God to be the kind of Father they can depend on without reservation.

Our children may get their view of God from us. Here are some pictures of God I want to make sure I am not painting:

A Stained-Glass God. Did your church building have beautifully colored glass windows — maybe picturing an ethereal-looking figure of Christ that hardly fit in the real world? Maybe those windows conditioned you to think of God as being separate from everyday life — some holy, spiritual, otherworldly being you could contact only in a religious location, such as a synagogue or a building with a steeple. If you were used to worshipping God in one of those locations, then you may be conditioned to think little about Him unless you are in such a building. You may think of God as living in a temple made by human hands and not as living within your heart.

An Absentee God. Many people see God as distant and uninvolved in our lives. Indeed, this is what the deists believe and teach — that God made all things and then left them to run on their own while he turned his attention elsewhere. Many people who are not deists, many Christians in fact, tend to think of God in this way. They feel that he is up there somewhere and that he sees us and knows what we're doing. But they have no relationship with him and think it's up to them to pull themselves up and perform well enough to earn his willingness to save them. The idea of a God they can relate to personally and intimately seems foreign to anyone with an absentee god.

A Scorekeeper God. People with this kind of god are continually burdened with guilt. He's up there looking down on you with a judgmental eye, ready to pounce the moment you get out of line. He has this great black book where he keeps a detailed record of everything you do, good or bad. When you get to heaven he will tally up both the good column and the bad. If your good deeds outnumber the bad, then he will let you in. But if not, well, you're in big trouble.

An OnStar God. This god is not with you every moment of every day in close relationship, but he is on call for the moment you encounter any situation you can't handle yourself. Just push a button and he is there to solve your problem, give you direction, or get you out of a jam. "This is god, what is your emergency?" Prayer is what pushes that button, which means you need not bother to pray until you have a need. In the days before electronics this god was called the "genie-in-a-bottle god," or maybe the "in-case-of-emergency-break-the-glass god."

A Grandpa God. Ahhh, but isn't this a pleasing picture? Many of us choose to believe in a god who just wants us happy. He never disciplines us, but turns his head when we do something wrong and smiles indulgently and forgives easily when we go astray. He gives us anything we ask for and just wants to be loved and to get along with everyone. He's a relaxed, benign, easy-to-please, available, rocking-chair kind of guy who loves to spoil us by giving us whatever we want. Come to think of it, this sounds likes me with my ten grandkids. When eleven-year-old Reagan looks at me with those endearing eyes, how can I say no? But her mom or dad can step in and stop my actions: "Dad, don't give her everything she asks for. We have to live with her."

Parent Point

The primary belief of the home is to love God with all of our hearts, souls, minds, and strength.

Guarding the Parent's Heart

Soon after you start humbling yourself before God as your King and you remain helpless, you have both the desire and ability to love God with all of your heart, soul, mind, and strength. That ability and desire has come to you from His gift of *grace* (love and power) as you remain "poor in Spirit." You are privileged to use His love, given only to the humble, to love Him back. You become continually aware that His kind of love comes only from Him alone (see 1 John 4:7-8). To love God with *all* of your *heart, soul, mind, and strength* involves understanding some of what each of these four words means.

Loving Him with All of Your Heart

Your heart contains all of your main beliefs. Your heart is like your main "control center." You are actually spiritually saved by God when you "say with your mouth" that Jesus is your King, Lord, and Master and "believe in your *heart*" that God raised Jesus from the grave (see Romans 10:9). For man *believes in his heart* and the result of believing that Jesus is Lord and that God's power raised Him from the dead is gaining God's righteousness. *Righteousness* is "thinking and acting as Christ did."

Daily, I seek His power by humbling myself in order to *desire Him* more than any of His creations: people, places, and things. As we desire to be with Him more than anything else, we are honoring Him, lifting Him up to the highest position in our life. We then tend to stop expecting anything on this earth to bring us any level of satisfaction compared to what God can do for us. He becomes your life, and therefore, you'll worship Him above all else. You can continue to enjoy any part of God's creation, but you can never worship any of it more than you worship God Himself. The balance of life is enjoying Him while you enjoy everything else. But never expect something from His creation that only He can give you.

This understanding of God's supreme value is one of the main keys to ending stress. When you stop expecting fulfillment from people, places, and things, and you start expecting God to meet all of your human needs, dreams, goals, and desires, you'll find that your stress level is much lower (see Colossians 3:1-3). Stress, or anger, is the gap between what you expect from God's creations and what you are actually receiving. The more you expect *all* of your meaningful life to come from God, the less stress you will experience. God is faithful to be with you always. He shepherds you beside still waters; He meets all of your needs through Christ Jesus. He is your comfort, strength, living water, and bread, front shield, rear guard, high tower. The list of who God is and what He does for us is endless![1]

The longer this trust in Him continues within you, the more you will begin to lose jealousy, greed, anger, envy, and the like (see Galatians 5:19-21). And the more of His love, joy, peace, patience, goodness, and the like will become who you are (see Galatians 5:22-23).

Loving God with all of your heart is craving Him day and night more than anything else on this earth with every living cell in your body. His righteousness (acting like God, loving, peaceful, patient, and so on) within you is always more precious than any stimulation or pleasure that you can gain from His creation. This is when you can have your cake and eat it too. Because when you seek God like you would cool water on a hot day, you get to live with God's power and love flowing through you and enjoy all of God's creation at the same time. When God satisfies you, you'll feel like saying, "Ahwwwwwww, that is so good and refreshing!"

Loving Him with All of Your Soul

Loving Him with all of your soul means loving Him with everything about you that is living. "And the LORD God formed man of the dust of the ground, and breathed into his nostrils the breath of life; and man became a living soul" (Genesis 2:7, KJV).When you desire God more than what you can gain from any of your five senses, you are loving from your soul. He's forever more valuable than anything you can experience on this earth.

Jesus said about our soul,

If anyone would come after me, he must deny himself and take up his cross and follow me. For whoever wants to save his life will lose it, but whoever loses his life for me will find it. What good will it be for a man if he gains the whole world, yet forfeits his soul? Or what can a man give in exchange for his soul? (Matthew 16:24-26)

Therefore, any of your five senses can be fulfilled by Him more than anything else on this earth:

Touch. Use the freedom that God gives us from His Spirit and the power of His Words living within us to love and serve others through touch. Let your touch be healing and comforting. Don't use the freedom He gives to think or act out using people for your own pleasures. Whatever you try to use for your own satisfaction, (creating things, hobbies, addictions) nothing on this earth will ever fulfill you like God can. Making things or enjoying hobbies will never compare to how He can meet your physical needs.

Sight. Lust of the eyes (material things, pornography) never compare to what He can give. It's okay to have cars, houses, money, and clothes but don't ever expect that any material thing on this earth can fulfill you. You can have nonstop pleasure from food, people, and so on, but don't seek fulfillment in life from any pleasures. Rather, live for and expect your true joy and fulfillment will come from God alone. Otherwise, things that bring you pleasure can become gods to you. Allow all the satisfaction you receive from the things of this world to be only overflow in your life.

Taste. Lust for food, drugs, and alcohol can never compare to Him. Seek Him with all of your heart in every way (see Colossians 3:1-5). Drink from Him the "living water" that allows you to never thirst again (see John 4:13-14). Again, let whatever this world has to offer be just your overflow from Him. Expect Him to fill you "to the measure of all the fullness of God" (Ephesians 3:16-20).

Smell. Food or the fragrances of this world can never compare to Him. The smell of the desert after a cool rain, the smell of flowers or honeysuckle, and all of the other wonderful aromas are just overflow compared to what He brings us. Our lives are a Christlike fragrance rising up to God. But this fragrance is perceived differently by those who are being saved and by those who are perishing (see 2 Corinthians 2:15).

Hear. Music and all other sounds can never compare to Him. The sound of the ocean, a sleepy brook, your favorite bird call — all of them don't come close to the sounds of His words being read aloud or His Spirit rushing into our hearts. No one will soon ask me to sing at a concert, but I do sing praises to Him many times per month. "May the words of my mouth and the meditation of my heart be pleasing in your sight, O LORD, my Rock and my Redeemer" (Psalm 19:14).

I continually meet people who turn things and other people into "little gods." With every one of our five senses, when we think that people can block our satisfaction from any one of these, are we not creating them into little gods? Nothing or no one can block what God has planned to give you or your kids!

Loving Him with All of Your Mind

Your *mind* is the king of everything about you. As a man "thinketh in his heart, so is he" (Proverbs 23:7, KJV). The greatest gift ever given to mankind is the ability to think and choose. Some experts say that your every thought creates and builds your beliefs, and after your beliefs are created by you, they are 10 million times more powerful than your mind at controlling your life. Beliefs might be a whole lot more powerful after they are created, but it's still the *mind* that is superior because it creates or recreates your beliefs. So, if you don't like some things about who you are, your mind can change your destructive, toxic beliefs. For example, if you are feeling lonely, sad, discouraged, fearful, or any of the hundreds of troublesome emotions, you can use your mind to form new beliefs that are consistent with Christ's truths. All of your thoughts can be conformed to Christ's words, and you can block all thoughts that do not conform to the eight approved thoughts in Philippians 4:8-9. Ask yourself, "Is what I'm thinking right now consistent to what is *true, honorable, right, pure, beautiful, lovely, excellent or worthy of praise?* Use these eight character traits as a guideline, and watch your beliefs change in a matter of weeks. I do this all day long, every day. We are to be transformed "by the renewing of [our] mind" (Romans 12:2). We're also instructed to, "Let this mind be in you, which was also in Christ Jesus." (Philippians 2:5, KJV). Guarding the heart is guarding our thoughts. Here is my paraphrase of 2 Corinthians 10:5: Take captive the thoughts on the Purple side, the thoughts of this world, and be obedient to Christ by thinking the thoughts He wants us to think, the four Red thoughts. And by thinking His thoughts, we build the powerful beliefs He designed us to have in our heart. Finally, we have a guarded heart full of His thinking, which leads us to the abundant beliefs. When we combine His beliefs in our heart with His Spirit within us, wow, do we have an overflowing life or what?!

Loving Him with All of Your Strength

Could the meaning be, "How you use your hands and feet to love and serve others"? Playing sports, building things, what you do on your jobs, or all of the things you do with your muscles and your actions. Don't even try to use your own power in using your arms or legs to find things that will bring fulfillment on this earth. Your hands cannot build things that are more important than your relationship with God. You certainly can build things that are overflow from the fulfillment of knowing and serving God's highest will for you: wanting Him more than anything and loving and serving others.

Nothing that you try to improve with your own abilities on this earth can give you any of His type of love, power, or fulfilling life that God can. God meets all of your needs. What does He want you to do in serving Him and others? What is His highest will for you? Isn't it to love Him and others? Are not all successful businesses finding what people need and meeting those needs in a quality way and servicing the products in an honoring way? One of the best parts of life for me is waiting on God to place a desire within me to show me what I can do in serving Him and others. He has always been faithful even up to my seventieth birthday this year. In fact, is it possible that God gave me this study you are now reading at my old age to show me what I've missed for so many years? I prayed and waited for over eight years to find peace about what God wanted me to do during my senior years. Many false callings came to me, and they never materialized. I just kept waiting on Him to guide me like the little widow lady in Luke 18. He eventually gave me this dream about memorizing and meditating on Scripture, and it seems like He opened all of the doors to make it happen.

Meditation Example

> Love the Lord your God with all your heart and with all your soul and with all your mind and with all your strength. (Mark 12:30)

To begin meditation, I say to myself, "Lord, I take all my affections, all my desires and needs and place them on your shoulders. You are everything that I'll ever need for my entire life. I have no expectations of high quality and lasting life from anything you created on this earth: people, places, or things. Nothing fills me like you do, God." I often jump to the first commandment, "And, Lord, you are my one and only God, above everything to me in value upon this earth." And then to the Lord's Prayer, "And also, God, you are my Father, how holy and lifted up to the highest value you are." Then, back to Mark 12:30, "Therefore, because I'm humble and you've blessed me with love and power, I do desire to love you, Lord. I want your beliefs, not my beliefs or the beliefs of the world. All my five senses, all my thoughts are honoring you, Lord."

I think through Philippians 4:8-9 to make sure that my thoughts are in line with Him. Some nights I go through all of my verses (see appendix). Every Bible verse I've memorized always fits within my four main Red Beliefs.

Then I go from the "mind" to my "strength." That's my feet and hands. I can spend two hours in the quiet of night meditating on my numerous Bible verses that keep reinforcing my beliefs to be in conformance to Christ's powerful and alive words. I not only love thinking His thoughts (my favorite Bible verses), but He is the one who gives me the desire to think on His words in the first place. Everything I have today is coming from Him. The power to humble myself comes from Him, after I humble myself before Him and others, He grants me more power and love to love Him and others. And finally, He gives me the power and desire to thank Him and even cheer for each and every hardship I experience. It's all about Him and it all comes from Him. I *think* on these types of *thoughts* every day. Thus, I build up His Red Beliefs and shrink the world's Purple Beliefs by refusing to think them longer than ten seconds.

Parent Plan

Paint a picture of God for your children.

Paint the God of miracles for your kids. I still don't understand how God does it, any more than I understand what's inside this computer and why I can send an e-mail to Russia in seconds. But I use my computer anyway. When God says He will be faithful to give His children whatever they ask in His name, that's what He means (see Mark 11:24). I just take it as fact and cooperate with my Creator by praying as He tells me to pray.

Paint the God of love for your kids. God made you and me so He could love us and love others through us. And He made us so we could return the same kind of love to Him. Had you thought of that? We were created to enjoy a personal, loving relationship with God and to find rich enjoyment in all creation.

The Scriptures affirm this idea everywhere:

I have loved you with an everlasting love. (Jeremiah 31:3)

So God created human beings in his own image. . . . Then God blessed them and said, "Be fruitful and multiply. Fill the earth and govern it." (Genesis 1:27-28, NLT)

God . . . richly provides us with everything for our enjoyment. (1 Timothy 6:17)

Even before the world was made, God had already chosen us to be his through our union with Christ. . . . Because of His love God had already decided that through Jesus Christ he would make us his children — this was his pleasure and purpose. (Ephesians 1:4-5, GNT)

He designed us to seek Him first and love Him with our whole heart, soul, mind, and strength. And when we do this, everything we need on this earth will be given to us. That's a powerful promise.

Think about how special we are in God's creation. He made us His deputies to rule the earth, and He intended for us to do it by the power of His Spirit living within us in a close, intimate relationship of love. We alone, out of all other creatures, are able to receive His love, pass it on to others, and love Him in return. That's our purpose for being. The whole idea boggles my mind.

Even more wonderful is the rest of the story. When man rejected God's love and turned away from Him, He was heartbroken, so He came after us. He came down and sacrificed Himself (Christ) on a cross to restore the loving relationship we had broken. Now we can reestablish that relationship and again enter into a loving bond with God. When we do this, we come to know and love God fully, and we begin to live in harmony with His purpose for us. Loving God produces the kind of joy He intended for us in the beginning.

Paint the God who became a man for your kids. The first verses of the book of John tell me that Jesus is God incarnate. Jesus is the Word, the essence of God revealed to us in human form. God became a man so that you and I could see in the flesh exactly what He is like. While on this earth, everything Jesus did was exactly what God the Father in heaven directed Him to do. The Word became flesh and dwelt among us. Is that amazing or what? (see John 5:19; 8:28).

We humans cannot completely understand the nature of God—how He can have three aspects—Father, Son, and Holy Spirit—and yet be one God. But then, why should we expect to understand Him? We are merely His creatures, and it would be strange if we understood everything about our Creator, wouldn't it? In fact, a God you could understand wouldn't be much of a God, because He would have to be small enough to fit inside your mind. But while we can't understand all about God, we can understand what He reveals to us about Himself. And He has revealed all we need to know. I like what the late Francis Schaeffer said: "We cannot know God fully, but we can know him truly."

Paint the God who has given us written instructions on how to live life for your kids. I find the Bible so dear and valuable because it is yet another evidence of how much God loves me. When I read the Bible, I can't help but love God in return. In loving Him, I become more like Him, which means taking those dear words He has given me and embedding them into my heart until they become a part of who I am. "Embedding His words in our heart" is simply thinking on the meaning of each word, over and over again, day after day, in a memorized Bible verse.

Memorize and Meditate

"The most important one," answered Jesus, "is this: 'Hear, O Israel, the Lord our God, the Lord is one. Love the Lord your God with all your heart and with all your soul and with all your mind and with all your strength.' The second is this: 'Love your neighbor as yourself.' There is no commandment greater than these." (Mark 12:29-31)

Do not conform any longer to the pattern of this world, but be transformed by the renewing of your mind. Then you will be able to test and approve what God's will is — his good, pleasing and perfect will. (Romans 12:2)

Dear friends, let us love one another, for love comes from God. Everyone who loves has been born of God and knows God. Whoever does not love does not know God, because God is love. (1 John 4:7-8)

Hear, O Israel: The Lord our God, the Lord is one. Love the Lord your God with all your heart and with all your soul and with all your strength. These commandments that I give you today are to be upon your hearts. Impress them on your children. Talk about them when you sit at home and when you walk along the road, when you lie down and when you get up. Tie them as symbols on your hands and bind them on your foreheads. Write them on the doorframes of your houses and on your gates. (Deuteronomy 6:4-9)

Loving God with Our Kids

Getting Started

Read Psalm 1:

Blessed is the man
    who does not walk in the counsel of the wicked
or stand in the way of sinners
    or sit in the seat of mockers.
But his delight is in the law of the LORD,
    and on his law he meditates day and night.
He is like a tree planted by streams of water,
    which yields its fruit in season
and whose leaf does not wither.
    Whatever he does prospers.

Not so the wicked!
    They are like chaff
    that the wind blows away.
Therefore the wicked will not stand in the judgment,
    nor sinners in the assembly of the righteous.

For the LORD watches over the way of the righteous,
    but the way of the wicked will perish.

What happens when you fill your mind and heart with God's Word?

What is the outcome of having our minds and hearts filled with the world's beliefs?

Introduction

In the do-it-my-way, tolerant, feel-good society that is prevalent today, the human tendency is for each person to make God into whatever he or she wants Him to be. I'm sure you've heard people say, "I just can't believe in a God who would send anyone to hell," or "I believe in a God of love, who just wants us all to be happy," or "I don't believe in a God who would give us so much pleasure in sex and then expect us not to enjoy it in any way we want." We tend to put self first, deciding how we think the world and our lives should be, and then we create for ourselves a god who approves it all.

You may not trust anyone but yourself. Like Sinatra, you may be determined to "do it my way" with no one telling you what to do or how to do it. If that's the case, you have made yourself your own god. I've tried this, and let me tell you, I make a lousy god.

Most of the religions of the world fall in one of two categories. In the first category, God is distant, and to please Him a person must perform certain actions and say certain approved words. People living under these religions fear being punished for any wrong acts or words. There is no personal love relationship between the people and their god. In the second category, God is loving, caring, and forgiving. He designed people to walk with Him daily in a love relationship. Only one religion falls into this category, and it happens to be Christianity. A follower of Christ is not so much in a "religion" with Christ, but in a personal, loving, caring *relationship* with Christ.

The God of Christianity sent His only Son to the earth to show us how to live. He came to suffer and die for our sins so that we are forgiven. And now He gives us His very Spirit to empower us to live the loving life He created us to live. God has given me the freedom to love Him and others as I want to be loved. Can you imagine living in a community where people are forgiving, gentle, kind, under control, loving, full of peace instead of stress, and more concerned about you than they are about themselves? That's true Christianity. What a new world we would have!

America is in trouble today because many people have lost their vision of God. But if we hide His commandments of love in our hearts, we will find that we are no longer automatically sinning against Him. I so desire this for America and the world. Christ said that if we let the world see the love we have for each other, they will know that our God is real.

Parent Point

I used to say to my kids when they were young, "What are the most important things in life?" I asked the question over and over again. Loving God and loving others are what Jesus called the most important commandments, but back then, I didn't know the importance of memorizing and meditating on God's words. But, do you know what? My kids can still tell you today in their late thirties and forties what they remember back then. Because I said it so many times, it was like I helped them meditate on God's truths in my own simple way.

Guarding the Parent's Heart

There are only two things on this earth that are eternal: people and the Word of God. Yet, how many of us live out our days focused on non-eternal matters? This life is not all there is.

I have many tasks and confrontational situations that seem to plague my schedule each week. To be honest with you, at one time I dreaded them. Now, I work at approaching each of them with an eternal perspective. In doing so, several key changes have taken place. First, I see that *issues* are not as important as *relationships*. Meaning, many of the issues that have bothered me are petty, trivial, and carry very little weight in light of God and eternity. But relationships are not petty. Can you discern between eternal and non-eternal issues?

When you live in light of eternity your values change. Your priorities are reordered. You use your time and energy more wisely. There's a higher premium placed on relationships and character rather than fame, wealth, or achievements.

God has a purpose for your life on earth, but it doesn't end here. First Peter 2:11 says that we are like aliens and strangers in the world. Therefore, we make the most out of our life here on earth as we prepare for our life beyond this one. It doesn't end here. This is our hope!

When we love God enough to put ourselves in His hands, He remakes us into something more wonderful than we could imagine for ourselves. He remakes us into His idea of what we should be, not our own. He remakes us into His own image. Think of it. Give yourself to God and you can become like God, reflecting His character and His glory.

When you fill your heart with His words, you push out your own self-serving beliefs that keep you bound to your lusts and desires for the things of this world. Instead of filling your heart with self, you fill it with God. He fills that empty space that has ached in the human heart since Adam and Eve kicked God out of their lives. As Blaise Pascal put it, it's a "God-shaped vacuum" that exists in every human heart. And it will remain unfilled until we fill it with God.

When we fill our lives with God, we fill our lives with love. That love never ends, but keeps pouring in. We find great joy when we spread that overflow of love into the lives of others. It fulfills our purpose. That's why the two greatest commands are to love God and love each other. That's what we're made for, and when you fulfill the purpose for which you're made, the result is more joy than you ever imagined.

Parent Plan

Pray regularly with your kids.

I never realized how much of an impact the daily prayers I had with my kids made on their lives. It was something I stumbled upon, but they have never forgotten the three most important things in life: Love God, Love others, and honor God's created things.

First Timothy 2:1 says, "I urge, then, first of all, that requests, prayers, intercession and thanksgiving be made for everyone."

What are some requests you need to bring before God as a family? Take time to acknowledge who God is. Pray through His attributes and names.

Who can you pray for? Pray for extended family, church members, and friends who do not know Jesus.

Spend time thanking God for who He is and the many blessings in your life. Make a list of the blessings.

Make a List of Ways to Love God As a Family
WITH ALL OF YOUR HEART (EMOTIONS)
What emotional pain can you express to God? How can you thank Him for sticking close through the pain?

What emotions can you validate in your children today?

What beliefs of the world (that live in your heart) are present in your house today? For example, do your children hear you saying, "We need a bigger house"; "We need more and better cars"? The Purple Belief thoughts of the world support the idea that unless you finally gain something — material things, a person, enough money—you'll not be happy or fulfilled. The world's Purple Beliefs will make you think that you don't have enough of something and if you had more of it, you'd truly be happy and content. That's a lie! Satan wants to "kill and steal and destroy" your life (John 10:10). He uses the things of this world to ruin you. If he can get you to believe you must have something or you'll be missing out, he's got you.

It's okay to have it all, but let your kids know that the only lasting satisfaction is knowing and loving God. Always capture the thoughts that tell you that you must have some material thing in order to have a higher quality of life. No, God is it and all you'll ever need. Seek Him first and last each day. Enjoy all that God has provided for you and your family, but never let the stuff you own replace your humility and love for God. And what is His purpose for you? To love others. How is He using you and your kids today to serve others? All full-time vocations are serving others in some way. Volunteering to help others in need is also loving God. When you love others, even the least of them, you are loving God (see John 14–15.)

What are some additional ways that your family will be loving God with all of your soul, mind, and strength?

Philippians 4:6-9 tells us what to think about to combat negative thoughts:

> Do not be anxious about anything, but in everything, by prayer and petition, with thanksgiving, present your requests to God. And the peace of God, which transcends all understanding, will guard your hearts and your minds in Christ Jesus.
>
> Finally, brothers, whatever is true, whatever is noble, whatever is right, whatever is pure, whatever is lovely, whatever is admirable—if anything is excellent or praiseworthy—think about such things. Whatever you have learned or received or heard from me, or seen in me—put it into practice. And the God of peace will be with you.

As you pray, write down thoughts that are:

True

Honorable

Right

Pure

Lovely

Admirable

Excellent

Praiseworthy

WITH ALL OF YOUR STRENGTH (BODY)
Are you getting enough rest?

Are you eating the right foods as a family?

Your body is a temple, and you love God with how well you take care of it. What lifestyle adjustments need to be made to better love God with your "temple"?

Memorize and Meditate

I tell you the truth, whoever hears my word and believes him who sent me has eternal life and will not be condemned; he has crossed over from death to life. (John 5:24)

The Spirit gives life; the flesh counts for nothing. The words I have spoken to you are spirit and they are life. (John 6:63)

To the Jews who had believed him, Jesus said, "If you hold to my teaching, you are really my disciples. Then you will know the truth, and the truth will set you free." (John 8:31-32)

Jesus replied, "If anyone loves me, he will obey my teaching. My Father will love him, and we will come to him and make our home with him. He who does not love me will not obey my teaching. These words you hear are not my own; they belong to the Father who sent me. All this I have spoken while still with you. But the Counselor, the Holy Spirit, whom the Father will send in my name, will teach you all things and will remind you of everything I have said to you. (John 14:23-26)

And without faith it is impossible to please God, because anyone who comes to him must believe that he exists and that he rewards those who earnestly seek him. (Hebrews 11:6)

Belief #3 — Love Others

Getting Started

Read 1 Corinthians 13:4-8:

> *Love is patient, love is kind. It does not envy, it does not boast, it is not proud. It is not rude, it is not self-seeking, it is not easily angered, it keeps no record of wrongs. Love does not delight in evil but rejoices with the truth. It always protects, always trusts, always hopes, always perseveres. Love never fails. But where there are prophecies, they will cease; where there are tongues, they will be stilled; where there is knowledge, it will pass away.*

List all the definitions of love in this passage.

What definitions of love are most evident in your home? Share one story of how love has been on display in your home this week.

Which of these definitions is missing in your home?

Can you make God's love shine from your life with your own efforts? Why?

Introduction

In the greatest sermon ever preached, the one Jesus delivered to a crowd gathered on the side of a Judean mountain, He said, "In everything, do to others what you would have them do to you, for this sums up the Law and the Prophets" (Matthew 7:12). This idea of loving others is a theme throughout the entire New Testament. Also, Jesus said that it sums up all God is telling us in the major books of the Old Testament. As I've mentioned in this study many times, loving God and loving others summarizes all of the Ten Commandments.

For a picture of just how God feels about our need to love others, look at the famous parable about the sheep and the goats (see Matthew 25:31-46). You know the story: When Christ returns He will judge all people, dividing them on His right and left as a shepherd divides his sheep from goats. He will send the "goats" on his left into eternal punishment. But those on the right will be given eternal life. And what was the basis for His approval? Here's how Jesus explained it:

> For I was hungry and you gave me something to eat, I was thirsty and you gave me something to drink, I was a stranger and you invited me in, I needed clothes and you clothed me, I was sick and you looked after me, I was in prison and you came to visit me. (Matthew 25:35-36)

The ones on His right were happy but surprised. They didn't remember ever seeing Jesus hungry or thirsty, needing clothing, sick, needing shelter, or in prison. So Jesus explained further:

I tell you the truth, whatever you did for one of the least of these brothers of mine, you did for me. (Matthew 25:40)

Do you get the picture? Every time we show love to another person, we show love to God Himself. He loves all of us so much and identifies with our needs so much that He makes no distinction between loving our fellow humans and loving Him. And according to this parable, loving others is so important to God that He makes it the primary criteria for judgment. It's not your correct theology that earns God's approval. It's not attending the right church. It's not performing all the right rituals in just the right way. The big thing in God's eyes is how much you love and serve your fellow humans. The apostle Paul said almost the same thing, "The entire law is summed up in a single command: 'Love your neighbor as yourself'" (Galatians 5:14).

The great disciple of love, John, amplified this idea in his first letter: "If anyone says, 'I love God,' yet hates his brother, he is a liar. For anyone who does not love his brother, whom he has seen, cannot love God, whom he has not seen" (1 John 4:20).

The greatest lesson that I have learned over these past few years is that of submitting to God's will of remaining humble in order to gain His love. I can now easily admit that God is responsible for all of what I do because He created every cell in my body. I can't take credit for anything, even loving others, because God is the one who saves me and empowers me with His love so that I can love and serve others. If I know Him and if I'm born of Him, then I gain His love and power to care for others (see 1 John 4:7-8).

In the previous session, we discussed why it is important to love God. He is worthy of love and service because of all He does for us. But why is it so important for us to love other people? What can they do for us? In fact, it often seems that other people are not doing things *for* us so much as doing things *to* us. What's the point of loving them? Well, it's really quite simple: If we are to be like God, we get to love like God. That means loving those He loves. Sometimes after introducing one of my friends to another friend, the first thing I hear is, "Any friend of Gary's is a friend of mine." That gets to the heart of why we should love other people. Any beloved of God's should be a beloved of ours. That means we must place the high value on all humans that He places on them. And again, we get to love them as He does. And the great part of this is that God gives us His love so that we can love others.

Parent Point

Love others as you would like to be loved with the power that only comes from God.

Guarding the Parent's Heart

After humbling yourself, you have both the desire and ability from His gift of love and power to love your neighbors as you love yourself. Without God's love flowing in and through you, mankind cannot fulfill the law of love for one another.

Almost every religion on earth has this third Red Belief, the Golden Rule, at the center of their beliefs or code of conduct. Love others in the same way that you want them to love you. It's called the "universal ethic." However, look at all of the suffering mankind continues to pile upon humanity. Where is this "loving others" action? It's only where you see God's love and power flowing from those who have tapped into His unlimited supply. And His love and power only comes to those who are humble, continually aware of their helplessness. When you are loving others, you are fulfilling the laws and prophets as it says in Matthew 7:12: "So in everything, do to others what you would have them do to you, for this sums up the Law and the Prophets."

This third Red Belief of "loving others" can be summed up from this section of Ephesians 3:

> I pray that out of his glorious riches he may strengthen you with power through his Spirit in your inner being, so that Christ may dwell in your hearts through faith. And I pray that you, being rooted and established in love, may have power, together with all the saints, to grasp how wide and long and high and deep is the love of Christ, and to know this love that surpasses knowledge — that you may be filled to the measure of all the fullness of God.
>
> Now to him who is able to do immeasurably more than all we ask or imagine, according to his power that is at work within us, to him be glory in the church and in Christ Jesus throughout all generations, for ever and ever! Amen. (verses 16-21)

Since God is the one who gives us His love and power after we humble ourselves, what does His love actually look like? According to 1 Corinthians 13, God's love is patient, kind, generous, grateful, humble, low-listed, mannerly, more concerned for others than self, not easily angered, very forgiving and not remembering the wrongs of others, doesn't want to do wrong things to others, gets excited about the truth, bears, believes, hopes, and endures all things. It never ends.

These loving qualities are yours as God's gift to you, and they will come to you as you remain humble before Him. Your main job is to remain helpless, crying out to Him to bring you His love and power. Then, it is a waiting time for you. Wait for His love with excited anticipation. Then, you will receive another blessing from God as a result of hungering and thirsting for righteousness, "for they will be filled" (Matthew 5:6).

If we are called to love our neighbors, we must ask the question, "Who is my neighbor?" We commonly think of neighbors as the people who live near us, but Jesus meant it to include all mankind—even our enemies. Jesus told His famous parable of the Good Samaritan to make it clear that "love your neighbor" means to love all persons, everywhere—not just our friends, allies, and countrymen.

With God's power and love flowing in and through you, it is very possible to love an enemy. It's important to realize that our enemies are typically people who have been wounded or are filled with anger themselves. It's easier to love someone who you understand has an "ouchie in his heart." That's what I used to say to my kids when some adult or another kid would try to offend them. Here is how God's Word says it:

> There is a saying, "Love your **friends** and hate your enemies." But I say: Love your **enemies!** Pray for those who **persecute** you! In that way you will be acting as true sons of your Father in heaven. For he gives his sunlight to both the evil and the good, and sends rain on the just and on the unjust too. If you love only those who love you, what good is that? Even scoundrels do that much. If you are friendly only to your friends, how are you different from anyone else? Even the heathen do that. But you are to be perfect, even as your Father in heaven is perfect. (Matthew 5:43-48, TLB)

When I meditate on 1 Corinthians 13:4-8, I say things like, *Lord, I can hardly wait to see more of your patience within me. Yesterday, I was short with my wife, and so today I'm so aware of my helplessness to have your type of patience. Please bring it so that my wife and friends can see it in me, and bring it to me in greater measure so that they get to feel a loving patience from another human. That way, they'll know that they too can have this gift from God as they wait upon you. I'll keep waiting, but I'm very excited to get it from you and I'll wait patiently! Lord, the same goes for your kindness, generosity, gratefulness, humility, the way you laid your life down for me and everyone else, your type of manners, and your deep concern for others. You were not easily angered, you are the King of forgiving and not remembering the wrongs of others, you never rejoiced when evil was being done, you were so excited about the truth, and you were always able to bear all things, believe all things, hope for all things, and endure all things. You never stopped loving us!*

I actually cry out daily for God to keep sending more and more of His love to me. His love is unlimited and eternal. It's broader than the heavens, deeper than the sea, higher than the sky, and longer than the universe. You and I will never gain all of God's love during our lifetime (see Ephesians 3:16-20). But, we can continue to gain more and more of it while we are alive. Also, the next belief, the fourth belief, will increase His love to you even more rapidly.

Parent Plan

We get confused about the meaning of love because we tend to want to connect the word with feeling affection for or liking another person. When we like someone or have genuine affection for him or her, we have no trouble having loving thoughts about that person. But when affection is not involved, we may be uncertain about how to love that person. How do I know I'm loving people for whom I have no liking or affection? For an answer let's turn to C. S. Lewis, who wrote so eloquently on the subject.

> Do not waste time bothering whether you "love" your neighbor; act as if you did. As soon as we do this, we find one of the great secrets. When you are behaving as if you loved someone, you will presently come to love him. If you injure someone you dislike, you will find yourself disliking him more. If you do him a good turn, you will find yourself disliking him less.[1]

Lewis shows us a great principle. It's hard to dislike someone when you do something good for him. The good deed is somewhat like an investment. When you expend time and energy on anything, you invest yourself in it, which increases its values in your eyes. Another way of seeing this action is to hope God has already given you enough love and you're testing the love waters in your heart. If it's already there, you'll want to continue loving a person or someone in need. Therefore, when you spend time and energy on behalf of another person, your estimation of the worth of that person increases. It follows that if that person is your enemy, your bad feelings toward him or her are likely to change to good feelings because you have invested something of yourself. Never forget that the real, alive, and wonderful love that God promises His humble followers is a gift from Him. You'll never be able to create it in your own effort. But you can keep testing to see if you have His kind of love by doing loving actions toward others, and if it's there in you, you'll know it because of the ease with which you show this love.

Who in your family needs more love from you this week?

What can you do for him or her to show your love?

Memorize and Meditate

You, my brothers, were called to be free. But do not use your freedom to indulge the sinful nature; rather, serve one another in love. The entire law is summed up in a single command: "Love your neighbor as yourself." (Galatians 5:13-14)

The second is this: "Love your neighbor as yourself." There is no commandment greater than these. (Mark 12:31)

Love is patient, love is kind. It does not envy, it does not boast, it is not proud. It is not rude, it is not self-seeking, it is not easily angered, it keeps no record of wrongs. Love does not delight in evil but rejoices with the truth. It always protects, always trusts, always hopes, always perseveres. Love never fails. But where there are prophecies, they will cease; where there are tongues, they will be stilled; where there is knowledge, it will pass away. (1 Corinthians 13:4-8)

You have heard that it was said, "Love your neighbor and hate your enemy." But I tell you: Love your enemies and pray for those who persecute you, that you may be sons of your Father in heaven. (Matthew 5:43-45)

Applying Our Love for Others

Getting Started

Read 1 John 4:19:

We love because he first loved us.

Where does love come from?

What are a few ways that our heart "closes," thereby making it impossible for us to receive God's love?

Introduction

World famous cardiologist Dean Ornish indicates throughout his book *Love and Survival* that if you are loving God and people well, you might be able to eat a little junk food once in a while and still remain healthy. He also shows a wealth of information about how loving God and others reduces your chances of major illnesses.[1]

God designed us to receive love and give love. When we don't follow His design, things start going wrong, emotionally, spiritually, and even physically. Life is love; everything else is just details.

No doubt you have encountered a number of people who even a mother can't love—difficult people you deal with on your job, in business relationships, in your church, in your immediate social circle, or even in your own family. No doubt you have been hurt by mean or uncaring people, people who deliberately cheated you, lied to you, undermined your projects, stood in the way of some cherished goal, or even caused injury or death to someone dear to you. Does God really expect me to love a person like that? Do I really have to love people who do bad things to me and hurt other people?

I have to tell you that the answer is yes. But the good news is that you can do it. In fact, whether you realize it or not, you are doing it already. You love one unlovable person whose life is filled with terrible deeds, attitudes, thoughts, and flaws that would make an angel blush. Who is that person? It's the one whose face you stare at every morning in the mirror. As Paul said, "After all, no one ever hated his own body, but he feeds and cares for it, just as Christ does the church—for we are members of his body" (Ephesians 5:29-30). We all love ourselves. Even when people commit suicide, they love themselves so much that they can't take the abuse they are receiving any longer, and they think it would be better for them if they were dead. That's just one example of how Satan lies to people and entraps them.

So admit it: you do love at least one imperfect person. In fact, loving yourself seems to be a logical necessity if we are to love others as we love ourselves. And the way you love yourself provides the key to the way you should love others. So let's look at just what it means to love yourself.

I'm sure that all your life you've heard the phrase "hate the sin, but love the sinner." That's the way you love yourself. You certainly don't like everything you do. You don't like the mistakes you've made, the habits you can't get rid of, the failure to control your lust, your temper, or your powerlessness against addictions. Yet in spite of these flaws and sins, you still want the best for yourself. In fact, the reason you hate these sins and weaknesses is that you know they are not good for you. They keep you from living the kind of life you want to live and being the kind of person you want to be. When you look at your own life, you understand your weaknesses and your desire to be better. You may not justify these weaknesses and sins, but you understand your struggle against them, and therefore, you forgive yourself for them. If you don't forgive yourself, you add more problems to your life. People who hate themselves can't even know God or know His love (see 1 John 2:9-11). You care for yourself in spite of your flaws. In other words, in this one particular case at least, you hate the sin and love the sinner.

This is exactly the way that God wants us to love others—as we love ourselves.

That is, we hate the sins and weaknesses that cause them to act obnoxiously or cheat or steal or harm, but we want the best for them. You want them to be rid of the motivations and deadly Purple Beliefs lodged in their hearts that make them act the way they do. You hate their toxic beliefs. You want them to have the peace and happiness they want as much as you want peace and happiness for yourself. You want them to have the essentials of life: clean water, healthy foods, warm and comfortable clothing, clear vision, and all of the other things you enjoy each day.

Here is how my granddaughter Hannah is keeping her heart open. Hannah is fourteen years old and as cute as a bug's ear. She was born premature and weighed less than two pounds. But today, she's alive and well. For the past year, I've been telling her that real beauty comes from a person's heart and that beauty shows through a person's eyes and facial expression. I have watched her realize that she is a "preemie" in her heart toward God. Preemies are very helpless and because she is so aware of her beginnings, she understands that if she keeps her heart open to God and realizes that only God gives real and genuine love, her own heart will be very beautiful little by little over the rest of her life. We pray for her future husband almost every day that he too will have a "preemie" heart toward God and that God is preparing him for a wonderful life with Hannah. She's watching for him every day.

Parent Point

Love others by keeping your heart open.

Guarding the Parent's Heart

The one Scripture that motivates me the most to serve others is Galatians 5:13: "You, my brothers, were called to be free. But do not use your freedom to indulge the sinful nature; rather, serve one another in love." Today I no longer use the freedom that Christ has given me to serve my own lustful or sinful pleasures. I think I'm 90 percent more free today than last year. But almost daily, God gives me some new insight to keep growing His beliefs and shrinking the world's beliefs. There is one thought that can creep into my mind from a past memory. Today, I realized that I can actually block this recurring memory by not entertaining it from the very first moment it enters my brain. Yaaaayyyy! Another victory for this day.

Before I got out of bed today, while meditating on my main Bible verses, the four Red verses, my thoughts were grateful and I was cheering for my failures yesterday. Once in a while, I still get thoughts that start to build from my youthful lust experiences. As they start to build in my mind, I can usually hold them long enough to start repeating the thoughts of my favorite verses. But yesterday one thought made it through all of my verses and kept moving in my mind long enough to cause me to feel defeated. But, right away I realized that my sins against the Lord are also my personal trials, just as the apostle Paul had some kind of "thorn in his side," a hurtful pain. Maybe it was also a temptation or recurring thought that plagued him? So I did what I do with all of my trials: I thanked God and cheered the pain and thought about the fact that today is the first day of the rest of my life. And God has always freed me before and He'll do it again. Someday, I'll get to the place where I have so much of His power and love that this old tempting thought will be gone. I know that this is so because of all of the freedoms and victories I've already experienced from Him. I have great hope, and failure does not get me down for very long because failure is one of my difficulties until I meet Him face to face.

When it comes to hope, can I share one other hope that I have with God? Jesus told us that His followers and those who believed in Him would do "greater things" than He did on this earth (John 14:12). Since He only speaks truth, that means that you and I someday will be able to touch someone's body and they will be healed of a sickness just as Jesus did. When? I don't know the date or time. But I do know that His promises are true. So from time to time, I pray for someone who is sick and ask God to reveal to me what His will is for this person. *Lord, is this the day that you'll heal this person through the power that lies within me from You?* I try it now and then, and so far I don't know of anyone who has been healed. My own wife has asked me to stop touching her knee and praying for healing because she seems to get worse after I pray. What's up with that? He is the one who heals us supernaturally and He may or may not use me, but I still try and check if His power within me is ready to heal.

I so enjoy using His freedom to keep loving others by serving them. And I willingly do this because His living, true, and powerful words have already reached my heart, and I review them every day. I absolutely love watching God's words changing me more into His image day after day. His words are really true: when I hide them in my heart, I no longer want to continue to sinning against Him. My relationship and dependence upon God gives me great hope for today and hopefully will for the rest of my life.

When we understand this deep reason behind our willingness to show love by serving, it makes loving others, even our enemies, much easier. When we think of God as our Lord, or Boss, or King, we are His servants. In the Old Testament a servant could love his master so much that he would make a commitment to serve him for the rest of his life. To ratify that decision the master would drive an awl (an instrument something like an ice pick) through the earlobe of the servant. From that moment on, the bondservant would wear an earring placed in the new hole in his ear. The earring would show that he was now totally surrendered to his master in the confidence that his master would treat him well.

If you are willing to become a bondservant of God, you can willingly serve others no matter what their return gesture may be. People can be frustrating and cruel, but as you remain humble before God, He will give you the powerful desire to love others when you otherwise could not do that on your own. Remember, you inherit the kingdom of God with all of its love and power to enable you to love people like you never imagined.

When your allegiance is to God, you can love even the unlovable. You can love them without any thought of what you might receive in return because you know that God fills you up with all the fullness of Himself. When you try to help others, they may judge your motives. Use God's power to help them anyway. If you succeed in life, you will win false friends and even enemies. Succeed anyway. Your good deeds of yesterday are already forgotten. Keep doing good anyway. As you help and serve others, they will often bite you and hurt you. Serve anyway. What they do and think does not matter. By serving them you are serving your God and showing them His unconditional loving nature. Just remember that it's God who rewards you and keeps you in His arms all the days of your life.

Parent Plan

Teach Your Children to Love Their Enemies

When it comes to the command to love, the Bible is very obvious in what is expected of Christians:

> Therefore, if you are offering your gift at the altar and there remember that your brother has something against you, leave your gift there in front of the altar. First go and be reconciled to your brother, then come and offer your gift. (Matthew 5:23-24)

When we get reconciliation from one who has been offended by us, we are usually confessing that our actions toward them were wrong and would they please forgive us? But we do our part in reconciliation no matter what response we might get back from the offended person.

It is next to impossible to have an open heart, receptive to God's will, if we are in serious conflict with others. God desires a sincere gift, not tarnished with unreconciled differences and past hurts. We are responsible to make sure people we have offended, or have been offended by, are freed from the bondage of anger, vengeance, or hate toward us.

So is anyone excluded from receiving our love? According to Matthew 5:44-48, even our enemies are worthy of our genuine love:

> But I tell you: Love your enemies and pray for those who persecute you, that you may be sons of your Father in heaven. He causes his sun to rise on the evil and the good, and sends rain on the righteous and the unrighteous. If you love those who love you, what reward will you get? Are not even the tax collectors doing that? And if you greet only your brothers, what are you doing more than others? Do not even pagans do that? Be perfect [mature], therefore, as your heavenly Father is perfect.

What a verse! Again, it touches on the very nature of our incredible God who is merciful and gracious to all. We are called to be perfect, "as your heavenly Father is perfect." Understanding that we cannot be completely perfect (mature) while existing on this planet, the verse is calling us to strive for Christ's perfection using His energy. We are daily being perfected, or made more complete or mature. Christ is willing to love those who were unlovable through us; to care for those who were prostitutes, thieves, and yes, even tax collectors; and to love those who most offend us. Why our enemies? God knows how much unresolved anger kills the spirit within, and He designed this command to help free us from eternal regret by reaching out to those who are filled with much anger and in darkness. Those hateful people are in a dark prison of anger and regret. Let's reach out to them before it's too late!

Teach your children to see the treasures from the pain they go through, mainly more of His love, but also, help your children understand that hurting people are in pain, and they don't realize it yet, but they have their own "hidden treasures" in their lives too. Never forget that "hurt people" hurt people. When people react to you, they are more than likely projecting pain. We have to love people beyond their words and actions.

Hide Words of Love in Your Heart

What kind of example do you display to your family, friends, strangers, to a rude driver who cuts you off in traffic, or to a sales clerk who cheated you at a store? How do you respond to people who offend you? As you carefully monitor how you act in these various situations, you'll see the patterns and habits that reflect the beliefs in your heart. Like me, you may have a belief in Jesus and even have memorized the great commandments of loving God and others. Yet you may still notice character qualities in your actions that do not reflect loving God and others on a consistent basis. Why? It's possible that you still have a throbbing portion of the toxic, deadly Purple Beliefs growing within your heart, even though you have planted the belief of loving God and loving others. Do all that you can every day to admit the size of your Purple Beliefs and hold the thoughts that build those toxic beliefs long enough to replace them with one or all of the Red thoughts!

We all have the seeds of the "deadlies" smuggled into our hearts by God's enemy. But we don't have to let them remain to sprout and take further root in our lives. I like the St. Augustine grass that grows so lushly on lawns in the South. When you set out that "carpet grass," as it is called, it will take over your yard if you water it regularly and feed it the right nutrients. Soon it will choke out all the dandelions and crabgrass. God's words are like that. Plant them in your heart and nurture them with the nutrients of daily meditation and study, and those seeds will grow each day within your heart and choke out the sprouts of the deadlies.

Which seeds are you mostly feeding in your heart—the deadlies or the words of God? It depends on which you water and nurture the most. If you allow the thoughts of pleasing yourself too often, the four toxic deadlies will take root, sprout, and choke out the things God desires in your heart.

As a reminder, the Purple Beliefs are what Satan wants you to believe, and they oppose Christ's belief of loving others like yourself. These Purple Beliefs include using people and things for your own personal pleasure, excitement, fun, or entertainment; using chemical stimulants to pleasure yourself; using people for sensual excitement; using animals or things to pleasure yourself; and a host of things that the world has discovered to bring additional pleasures that usually end in addictions or slavery. Just think about the trafficking of humans today. Why? So that men can be more pleasured. When our hearts are filled with the world's beliefs, we see all manner of evil in the actions of men and women.

Maybe you have been feeding your deadly beliefs for so long that they have grown deep roots and tall branches. The good news is that you can start choking off any beliefs you want by beginning to meditate on the thoughts of God's Word in the four Red Beliefs. As you feed the "love God and others" thought seeds, your heart will soon be filled with the healthy growth of your character, conforming more and more into the image of God. That will lead you to becoming more caring and loving. The words of God in the Bible are alive and powerful. They can change your beliefs. Think regularly on the love passages of the Bible and the seed will continue to grow deeper roots and larger branches until it becomes like a tree planted by the rivers of water, and the leaves never wither again. When that tree becomes firmly rooted in your heart, you will come to love naturally and automatically because whatever strong beliefs you plant in your heart determine what you think, say, do, and feel. Dr. Caroline Leaf tells us in her book *The Gift in You* that the very acts of love start destroying the Purple Thoughts and Beliefs logged within your heart. Any loving thoughts begin to "break off" the damage done to our brain by the Purple Thoughts and Beliefs.[2]

Ideas for Seeing God's Word Everywhere

- Write a verse on your bathroom mirror with a grease pen.
- Take a washable Sharpie to the bedroom wall (parent's permission required).
- Turn verses into songs. (My wife loves doing this!)
- Write and memorize poems with sections of Scripture.
- Create artwork and hide verses in a frame or objects.
- Add a verse to your computer's screensaver.
- Post verses on your child's Facebook wall.
- Text verses to your children throughout the day.
- Scribble Bible verse references on the inside tags of your child's clothes.
- Write them on small plaques near the walkway into your house.
- Buy T-shirts that have Scriptures written appropriately within a design.
- Sing the songs that reflect God's love and His words.
- Write Scripture verses on the bottoms of your shoes.
- Put Scripture on small note cards taped to your car dash.

What other creative ways to hide God's Word can you think of?

Memorize and Meditate

Dear friends, let us love one another, for love comes from God. Everyone who loves has been born of God and knows God. Whoever does not love does not know God, because God is love. (1 John 4:7-8)

We love because he first loved us. If anyone says, "I love God," yet hates his brother, he is a liar. For anyone who does not love his brother, whom he has seen, cannot love God, whom he has not seen. And he has given us this command: Whoever loves God must also love his brother. (1 John 4:19-21)

Love the Lord your God with all your heart and with all your soul and with all your mind and with all your strength. (Mark 12:30)

That if you confess with your mouth, "Jesus is Lord," and believe in your heart that God raised him from the dead, you will be saved. For it is with your heart that you believe and are justified, and it is with your mouth that you confess and are saved. (Romans 10:9-10)

Let us not love with words or tongue but with actions and in truth. This then is how we know that we belong to the truth, and how we set our hearts at rest in his presence whenever our hearts condemn us. For God is greater than our hearts, and he knows everything. (1 John 3:18-20)

To the Jews who had believed him, Jesus said, "If you hold to my teaching, you are really my disciples. Then you will know the truth, and the truth will set you free." (John 8:31-32)

Be devoted to one another in brotherly love. Honor one another above yourselves. (Romans 12:10)

Belief #4 — Rejoice in Trials

Getting Started

Read Romans 5:3-5 and James 1:2-4:

> Not only so, but we also rejoice in our sufferings, because we know that suffering produces perseverance; perseverance, character; and character, hope. And hope does not disappoint us, because God has poured out his love into our hearts by the Holy Spirit, whom he has given us. (Romans 5:3-5)

> Consider it pure joy, my brothers, whenever you face trials of many kinds, because you know that the testing of your faith develops perseverance. Perseverance must finish its work so that you may be mature and complete, not lacking anything. (James 1:2-4)

What are some trials you have experienced in your lifetime?

How does the world teach us to respond to trials?

How does James teach us to respond?

What does Romans 5 teach us we will receive from trials?

Introduction

A heart research group in California has found that an attitude of gratefulness is extremely beneficial to human health. With every thought of gratitude and thankfulness, healthy chemicals are released into the body. On the other hand, with each negative, critical, or worrying thought, the body is flooded with harmful chemicals that can damage one's emotional and physical health.

This study supports the premise of this entire book. If you change the belief in your heart from worry-producing, negative thoughts to positive, grateful thoughts, it will improve your mental and physical health. It will improve your life.

For the most part, the stressful, traumatic, and trying events that happen to us produce these negative thoughts, which can result in resentment and worry. Wouldn't you love to find a way to rid yourself of such thoughts? Wouldn't you love to change the beliefs in your heart so that instead of feeling anger, resentment, revenge, worry, complaining, or stress because of your trials, you experience more love and joy because of your difficulties? It's possible, believe it or not. And this is not just my idea: I learned it from the apostle Paul. He told us to stop worrying and find peace (see Philippians 4:4-7). But how?

Just recently I had another chance to learn this principle. I face just as many frustrating experiences as you, but over the past couple of years I have finally come to the place where my trials do not "do me in." I have replaced resentment and worry with gratefulness. In fact, amazing as it seems, I now find joy in my trials. Seem impossible? Not at all. In this session, I will show you how.

Parent Point

We cannot protect our children from all difficulties and pain, but we can help them process through it.

Guarding the Parent's Heart

After humbling yourself continually, you will have His power and love to experience everything and anything that happens to you with a heart of thanksgiving. You normally won't feel grateful *during* the suffering. While hardships are happening to you, you'll eventually find the strength and ability to think grateful thoughts even in the midst of pain. You will be able to understand and see God's power and love at work within you.

As you are being empowered by God, you will start seeing how all trials, difficulties, hardships, and tough times have "spiritual gems." This is one of the most important truths or beliefs that a follower of Christ can embrace.

As this belief grows within you through your grateful thoughts by quoting your favorite "trial" Bible verses back to God, you will soon understand that all difficult times have a real silver lining. Your children will see such a change in you that they will naturally want to model their lives after yours!

There are pearls in every crisis. You will wind up each day with either good things or bad things happening to you. But after a short time, in most cases, you'll begin to see a benefit in each bad experience. And, eventually, you'll get better and better at trusting the results of all trials to bring you benefits over time. All negative things happening to you will bring you something good or great. Once your meditation on verses like Romans 8:28 reach your heart as a belief, you'll start seeing your trials as your friends.

Why does the Word of God tell us that all trials and difficulties are experiences that we can boast about with joy?

> Consider it pure joy, my brothers, whenever you face trials of many kinds, because you know that the testing of your faith develops perseverance. Perseverance must finish its work so that you may be mature and complete, not lacking anything. (James 1:2-4)

You become more and more mature with the increased love you receive from God, and your trials of *all* types will refine both your love and power that was given to you by Him. Is that promise amazing or what?

After a while, you'll start believing that in every circumstance you will come out smelling like a rose. There are only three bad things that can happen to a follower of Christ, and all three are good to great for you:

1. Just being human, life can beat you up in all kinds of ways. But after being beat up and remaining humble, expressing thanksgiving to God, you will receive more love and power from God. "Boast about your trials because you are instantly gaining more of His endurance, more of His character qualities, more hope. And hope is never disappointing because the love of God is being poured into your *hearts* by the Holy Spirit" (Romans 5:3-5, paraphrased).
2. Life can beat you up until you are in a coma. You're asleep, and if you wake up, you'll either be in category 1 or 3.
3. Life can beat you up to the point that you have passed on to the presence of God in heaven. That's great because now you are with God for eternity!

Therefore you can boast about your difficult gifts from God, for all good things come from God. And as life throws you anything negative, you can expect everything to turn into good or great. So, I always say, "Life, bring me the good or the bad. I will benefit either way." And I actually benefit even more from the bad. I'll rejoice, and again I say that I will rejoice in everything that happens to me. Everything works together for my good because I love God (see Romans 8:28). I've been empowered to love others, and then I'm empowered to thank God in all circumstances because I know that the pain of trials leads me to loving Him and others more. I'm being refined by trials like gold. Then, I get more trials so that I'm polished so you can see God's reflection in my actions. Nothing is wasted on me, I'm never a victim. I truly can give thanks for all things for this is God's will through Christ Jesus (see 1 Thessalonians 5:18).

I'm now seventy and more excited today about seeing God working through me in the future than at any time before. My life is just starting, because every day is the first day of the rest of my life! I live with great hope about today and tomorrow. What will He inspire me to do today? How will He use me today and tomorrow? All things are possible through Him. I get to discover His dreams for me and what it is He wants to do through me. And as life gets difficult, I get even better at serving Him and others. Hallelujah!

Always remember that a grateful heart is not only a happy heart but a healthy life. An angry, judgmental, negative, critical heart releases harmful hormones into your body that greatly damage it. But a grateful heart releases health-giving hormones. I'd much rather be a thankful person in all circumstances than a negative, critical, or sickly person. This is possible as I remain humble while receiving His power and love flowing in and through me during all difficulties that I face. I have almost come to a place where I can block all negative thoughts about trials as they are hitting me. I am taking all negative thoughts captive to make them obedient to Christ (see 2 Corinthians 10:5).

Here are some examples of benefits that come after hard times:

I was forced out of a wonderful job at age thirty-five. It hurt like crazy. I couldn't eat for days; I was very angry and deeply hurt. I wanted revenge. My thoughts were constantly negative and wondering where God was in all of this mess. But after two years of grieving, I finally forgave the person and started realizing how much I was like that person and God seemed to purify me of my self-centered lifestyle. I understood more clearly how divorced people hurt deeply. After I forgave the person, it was as if God opened my eyes and started leading me into helping couples and families in pain. My entire ministry grew out of the pain of leaving that former ministry. I look back on it and it has become my very favorite memory because of all of the good that came to me as a result.

I had a heart attack and kidney transplant over nine years ago and I have received amazing benefits. That's when I finally began learning that I had been managing God's rewards and walking away from the Rewarder. I came to know the great value of His written words. I understood that they are alive and sharper than a two-edged sword. This study is the result of the pain I endured. Pain is a wonderful gift and when your heart is filled with this belief. You, too, can view trials from an entirely new, wonderful perspective.

After all of the years that my family camped together, we finally came to the conclusion that camping is scheduled disasters. The hardship of camping together is an event that brings families into a closer unit. The pain you experience together and the anger toward each other that is later forgiven knits your family together. My kids and I are still very close as a result of camping for fifteen years during their youth.

Meditation Example

Here's what you can say back to God while any trial and hardship is weakening you:

> Your grace is always sufficient for me, Gary Smalley, for your power, Lord, is perfected in my weakness. Most gladly, therefore, I am boasting about my weaknesses, so that your power, Christ, may dwell in me. Therefore I am well content with weaknesses, with insults, with distresses, with persecutions, with difficulties, for your sake, Christ; for when I am weak, then I am stronger in you! (2 Corinthians 12:9-10, paraphrased and personalized)

I regularly pray, "Lord, each day I have my share of hardships and conflicts with people. Thank you today for the negative things that happened to me. (I actually list them for God. For example, today with icy roads in our town, my flight may not leave on time and my wife heard some very discouraging news.) I feel terrible about what has happened to me and about those I have offended, but through these difficult circumstances, I now understand and know that you are perfecting the power and the love you have placed within me. I may not see the benefits today, Lord, but I know I will in a short time. Lord, you have never let me down, but you have always shown me more of your love within. Sometimes, you have given me much more than I expected. You are adding more of your love within me right now through my pain. I don't like to be weakened by trials, Lord, but thank you that you can use them now for my good. Today is not going to be an exception with me. You have always given me treasures from each and every trial. So I end this day by thanking you over and over again for how wonderful you are to enrich my life through the trials I faced today and every day in the future. I can't watch the refining process now, but I know that it is going on within me, and I'm looking forward to viewing it someday."

It is my continual prayer for you that God's words sink deep within your heart and develop into very large, grateful beliefs. As the Bible verses you memorize reach your heart through meditation, may you be as grateful as I am for having a God who cares enough to guide us each and every step of our life by His words living within us.

Parent Plan

Basically, no trial, difficulty, or hardship is inherently good. The loss of a loved one is not good, and a physical injury is a bummer. They are all bad, and we wish we could have avoided them. But the truth is that we can't. We don't have to *like* any trial, but the great worth of every trial is our ability through Christ's power given to us to view the trial as a gift, a great future earning, a treasure in time, or a huge benefit within days of experiencing a hardship. It's our amazing gift from God that we humans can think what we want to about any trial. We can choose to accept the reality that any and all difficulties will bring us something good after a while. If God tells us that He can cause *all* things to work together for our good, if we are loving Him and others, then that's the belief I want in my heart. In fact, I have that belief within me now. That's why I rarely complain or worry anymore. After a few hours or days of grief over a loss or injury, we have the power from God to actually thank Him and cheer for our difficulties because each one of them will bring us wonderful benefits in time. I call this phenomenon "treasure hunting" a bad experience to find the good. And the good will always contain some new quality of God's love living within us.

When a trial hits us, we don't have to blindly search for the treasure within it. I have discovered two specific steps we can take to locate the gems pretty quickly and guide our children into rejoicing in trials. Let's look briefly at these steps:

1. As soon as the trial hits you, validate the pain and teach your children how to start giving thanks for the pain.
Whether your trial involves mental stress or physical pain, it's the emotional pain that actually does the work toward remolding you into the image of God. The essence of His image is love, so start looking for the different expressions of love that are moving into your life while the pain lasts.

I think that is why James tells us to "Consider it pure joy [deposit joy into your heart's bank before you actually reap the benefit], my brothers, whenever you face trials of many kinds, because you know that the testing of your faith develops perseverance. Perseverance must finish its work so that you may be mature and complete, not lacking anything" (James 1:2-4). James is telling us to let the pain continue until it makes us "mature and complete." When you are "complete" you have all of the love you can gain from the pain of the current trial. When you reach this completeness, the pain will stop. This means as long as the pain continues, you must keep searching for the results and the results come more quickly from a grateful heart than they do from anger and resistance.

2. Help your children look deeply for the "love gold" to be found within each difficulty.
The "love gold" shows itself in the following ways:
Empathy. My painful experience has given me a much deeper sensitivity to the pains of others.

Compassion. Now I can feel real love and compassion for hurts of all kinds in other people, especially those who cannot find relief for their pain.

Sensitivity. After experiencing my own bout with pain, I find that I can sense more acutely when a hurting person needs a word of encouragement or a helping hand.

Humility. When you have been through continuous pain, you understand the helplessness one feels when facing a difficulty that has no solution. That's when we learn humility—we understand that we are helpless without God. At that very moment, He is giving us even more of His love and power.

As you continue thinking the thoughts of God's words concerning hardships of all kinds, you'll come to the wonderful place of actually rejoicing, *cheering,* for your hardships. As the grateful belief continues to grow within your heart, you and your children will be amazed at the change in your thoughts about trials.

Memorize and Meditate

Blessed are those who are persecuted because of righteousness, for theirs is the kingdom of heaven. Blessed are you when people insult you, persecute you and falsely say all kinds of evil against you because of me. Rejoice and be glad, because great is your reward in heaven, for in the same way they persecuted the prophets who were before you. (Matthew 5:10-12)

Consider it pure joy, my brothers, whenever you face trials of many kinds, because you know that the testing of your faith develops perseverance. Perseverance must finish its work so that you may be mature and complete, not lacking anything. (James 1:2-4)

Give thanks in all circumstances, for this is God's will for you in Christ Jesus. (1 Thessalonians 5:18)

Not only so, but we also rejoice in our sufferings, because we know that suffering produces perseverance; perseverance, character; and character, hope. And hope does not disappoint us, because God has poured out his love into our hearts by the Holy Spirit, whom he has given us. (Romans 5:3-5)

And we know that in all things God works for the good of those who love him, who have been called according to his purpose. (Romans 8:28)

But he said to me, "My grace is sufficient for you, for my power is made perfect in weakness." Therefore I will boast all the more gladly about my weaknesses, so that Christ's power may rest on me. That is why, for Christ's sake, I delight in weaknesses, in insults, in hardships, in persecutions, in difficulties. For when I am weak, then I am strong. (2 Corinthians 12:9-10)

Rejoicing with Our Kids During Trials

Getting Started

Read 2 Corinthians 12:9-10:

> But he said to me, "My grace is sufficient for you, for my power is made perfect in weakness." Therefore I will boast all the more gladly about my weaknesses, so that Christ's power may rest on me. That is why, for Christ's sake, I delight in weaknesses, in insults, in hardships, in persecutions, in difficulties. For when I am weak, then I am strong.

What happens when we show signs of weakness?

How should we respond to our weakness?

What does culture teach us to do with weakness?

Introduction

It excites me to see all the areas of life in which love provides the answers. If you apply the principle of love even when dealing with trials or difficulties, the problems turn into blessings. First, I humble myself before God and gain His powerful love so that I can even love the people who offend me most often. Second, I love God. I trust Him to bring good out of every trial when I open my heart to the blessings that come from enduring with patience and hope. Third, I love my neighbor and my enemy. Suddenly my trials are no longer trials. They are character-strengthening exercises that make me more into the glorious creature that God intends me to be.

I used to wonder about the apostle Paul. How could that man possibly be so happy with all the terrible troubles he went through? From the moment he became a Christian, trouble dogged him like a hive of mad hornets. He was distrusted; people tried to kill him in all kinds of ways; the Romans beat him several times; he was stoned, run out of town, often put in prison chains; and he survived shipwrecks and a venomous snakebite. And on top of all that he endured some kind of health problem, a "thorn in his side" that often hampered his work. Yet you could never find a more upbeat, joyful, and utterly dedicated man. This guy was sold out to the Lord, and he seemed to love every minute of it. Not only did he rejoice in his suffering, he rejoiced just for the love of his Lord: "Rejoice in the Lord always," he wrote. "I will say it again: Rejoice!" (Philippians 4:4). *Rejoice* means to return to the source of your joy. And that word keeps popping up in all of Paul's writings. The man was irrepressible. And right after telling us to rejoice, he wrote, "Give thanks in all circumstances, for this is God's will for you in Christ Jesus" (1 Thessalonians 5:18). Did you pause on the words, "thanks in *all* circumstances"?

But I don't wonder about Paul anymore. Now I understand. When I grow up, I want to be like Paul. He knew that his trials were the hammer and chisel of the Master Sculptor, chipping away at him and forming him into a copy of the One he loved more than anything in the world. Every trial, every difficulty, every bad time, every experience of being cheated, ripped off, put down, or beat up gives you another opportunity to win that trophy. Accept difficulties joyfully and with thanksgiving and they will open your heart to receive more of God's character — His patience, His compassion for others, His strength in your weak places, and His great and mighty love.

When you think of trials as blessings, it turns your attitude toward them completely on its head. With that trophy waiting to be awarded, how can children of God remain upset when trials start hitting them? I understand that now. But if trials hit you and your heart is not prepared with the right beliefs about them, you will not see them as blessings. You will see them as burdens, as blights on your life, and they will wear you down and, most likely, lead you to an earlier death.

Parent Point

Validate your child's pain and treasure hunt for the "pearls" in the trials after a time of allowing grief.

Guarding the Parent's Heart

Life for me is an adventure, and I've found that I live it to the fullest by finding the positive within each negative. I'm not saying that the very moment a negative experience hits me I immediately see the gem within it and welcome it with open arms. I'm not perfect yet. But since I put into my heart the scriptural principles of rejoicing in trials, I realize that every trial is an exercise machine to produce stronger character. I'm now able to manage the negative emotions with the belief that "in all things God works for the good of those who love him, who have been called according to his purpose" (Romans 8:28). And what is His purpose for me? To love Him and love others. Now every blow that hits me increases my love for Him and others. And whatever negative emotions I have at first are eventually transformed into joy. I have never experienced an exception.

You may think you have experienced exceptions. You may have suffered devastating, soul-wrenching blows that you are convinced could not possibly have any positive value. You may even feel insulted by the suggestion that it could. "How dare you think I could possibly rejoice in the death of my son!" Don't misunderstand me; I'm not claiming that every experience is good. Death is horrible. It can be an insult to God's creation, and He hates it so much that He died to kill it. Yet, even from such a terrible experience, great good can come, though the good may not be immediately apparent. The bottom line with great trials is that we can either thank Him for the pain or we call Him a liar because "no possible good could come from my giant trials." As hard as it is to thank God during difficult times, God is still alive and concerned for you, and He can take your pain and turn it into golden love in time. He doesn't lie!

No one can be expected to immediately find a blessing in the death of a loved one. Death inflicts a major wound that will take time to heal before you find the pearl that can grow from the pain. You can grieve your loss for weeks, months, or years, but eventually, God will be faithful and show you how you are more loving because of your pain. Yet, let me assure you that every trial—from minor irritations such as a cold, bad weather, problems with your house, with your job, illnesses, all the way to the loss of a loved one or your own impending death—has within it a gem just waiting to be found. In my seventy years, I've never seen one exception!

Here is the downside when you don't seek the gem within each trial: You must deal with the trial on its own terms, which means you must see it only as a problem, and possibly an insurmountable one. Mind you, I'm not saying you shouldn't deal with the problem. You must seek a cure for your health issue. You will have to repair the roof after the tree fell on it. You will have to come to terms with the loss of your loved one. Finding the gem within trouble does not eliminate the trouble itself. But what it does is give you a positive outcome from the negative experiences. This can make a huge difference. It's often the difference between hope and despair, love and loneliness, peace and anguish. If you see nothing in the trial but the difficulty, the pain, or the tragedy, you have no way to look up. Hope is lost. You are stuck inside the problem with no windows to let in sunlight.

But when you seek the gem within the trial, which, of course, is the ability to use the trial to build your character into the image of God, you don't have to let the difficulty grind you down or sink you into despair. In fact, when you gradually develop your own deep belief from Bible verses such as 2 Corinthians 12:6-10, you'll begin to see your troubles as blessings in disguise. Everyone needs *hope* within his or her troubles. God gives that hope when you know that something good is going to happen to you as a result of the pain. And the good can come to you in any number of ways or benefits. It's not limited to better character. I have received money, property, additional friends, new jobs, a new house, awards, and many other varied surprises.

The Purple Belief from Satan about trials is: All trials and difficulties are to be avoided and are bad for me. He wants you to think horrible thoughts like, *Why me, God? No, I can't be fired from this job, that would be a massive downfall, I'm ruined, I'm a failure, I'm stupid to have done that, I'll never amount to anything, I'm useless, my life is too hard, I can't take this pain any longer, I'm depressed, I want to end my life, no one cares for me, I'm all alone against my enemies, I'm no good, I'll get revenge.* Trust me, there are many more negative outcomes from believing that trials are bad for me. As I've said, most of the evil that occurs in our world comes from all four of the Purple Beliefs.

Parent Plan

Validate Your Child's Pain

Communication and listening to your child's feelings are at the heart of validation. Let them share how they feel without interrupting with comments such as, "Remember, this is actually good for you." The amazing truth about trials is that, if used correctly, they allow you to validate your child by listening to and understanding their pain. Validation simply means that you value a person's opinions, ideas, concerns, needs, and feelings. It doesn't mean that you have to agree with what your child is saying, but you give them a sense that you really "get" them. Allow hours or even days before trying to help them "treasure hunt" for the good benefits in trials. James 1 tells us to let the painful process take its full course. Don't rob your children of pain because it is like cheating them. During a trial, either you can force them to get over it or you can provide them with an experience of being heard and understood. The latter option is validation. When you validate someone, you don't instruct or try to change what he or she is feeling; instead, you seek first to understand. Memorize and use James 1:19-20: "Be quick to listen until you understand, keep quiet and therefore, you'll be slow to anger. Anger never brings about the righteousness of God" (paraphrased).

When you are able to validate someone, he or she should walk away with a very clear message: "My feelings are valuable." What a tremendous gift! Can you think of feelings that your children have tried to express, and rather than validating them you excused them or explained them away, or worse, said something like, "Oh, you big baby"?

When was the last time you simply embraced your spouse when he or she was sharing frustrations, rather than trying to solve the problem?

Cheerlead with Your Kids Through Trials

Rejoicing and boasting about trials is to find some pom-poms and start saying, "Yeah!" Although it may take time to work up to thanking God for *everything*, gratefulness allows us to see our relationship with Him in the proper perspective.

We will understand our great need for God and stay humble before Him and the people around us. Let's be a blessing to God and others as we focus on developing and expressing a heart of thanksgiving. Cheerleading a major trial will only come sincerely after a major, larger belief is within your heart that trials will in time bring me big benefits. I'll cheer now even if I'm still hurting only because I know the great good is coming soon.

Start a Gratitude Box

At dinner pass around some index cards and ask each member of the family to write down two or three things they are grateful for. Then place the cards in a box. While you have your kid's attention, take the cards out and read them before the whole family. You'll be amazed at how Mom and Dad can help kids treasure hunt after they have thought about the trials during the week.

Start a Benefit Box

Same exercise, but this time you are going to write down and share your most pressing trials. One at a time, share the trials. Help your kids learn how to validate each other. Allow each member of the family to give perspective to the trial. With this, you comfort one another through the trials. Then, during the day or night, any family member can write down thoughts on some of the benefits that will be coming to the person with his or her unique shared trial.

Memorize and Meditate

Blessed are those who are persecuted because of righteousness, for theirs is the kingdom of heaven. (Matthew 5:10)

Be joyful always; pray continually; give thanks in all circumstances, for this is God's will for you in Christ Jesus. (1 Thessalonians 5:16-18)

Do not be anxious about anything, but in everything, by prayer and petition, with thanksgiving, present your requests to God. And the peace of God, which transcends all understanding, will guard your hearts and your minds in Christ Jesus. Finally, brothers, whatever is true, whatever is noble, whatever is right, whatever is pure, whatever is lovely, whatever is admirable — if anything is excellent or praiseworthy — think about such things. Whatever you have learned or received or heard from me, or seen in me — put it into practice. And the God of peace will be with you. (Philippians 4:6-9)

And we know that in all things God works for the good of those who love him, who have been called according to his purpose. (Romans 8:28)

But he said to me, "My grace is sufficient for you, for my power is made perfect in weakness." Therefore I will boast all the more gladly about my weaknesses, so that Christ's power may rest on me. That is why, for Christ's sake, I delight in weaknesses, in insults, in hardships, in persecutions, in difficulties. For when I am weak, then I am strong. (2 Corinthians 12:9-10)

Consider it pure joy, my brothers, whenever you face trials of many kinds, because you know that the testing of your faith develops perseverance. Perseverance must finish its work so that you may be mature and complete, not lacking anything. (James 1:2-4)

Stay the Course

Getting Started

Read Ephesians 6:4:

> *Fathers, do not provoke your children to anger, but bring them up in the discipline and instruction of the Lord.* (NASB)

How do you "provoke your children to anger"?

Can you name a few times when you said or did something that provoked your children?

How did you restore the relationship?

Introduction

When we provoke our children, we "close their hearts" because of anger. More than anything, you want your child to have an open heart toward God and others. Throughout this study, we have learned about four beliefs every child needs. They cannot receive those Red Beliefs when their hearts are closed. If their hearts close and stay closed, then, tragically, the world's beliefs will find themselves a home and get comfortable inside of them.

Twenty Consequences of a Closed Heart in Your Child

1. Your child can begin to avoid and resist you.
2. Your child may resist activities you like.
3. Your child may purposefully choose friends you will disapprove of.
4. Your child will not love God.
5. Your child will not love God's Word.
6. Your child will leave the church upon leaving home.
7. Your child will abandon your values.
8. Your child moves toward darkness.
9. Your child creates distance or isolation with you or other believers.
10. Your child experiences more immoral temptations while remaining in the spiritual darkness.
11. Your child has diminished sensitivity and interest in touch.
12. Your child shows signs of depression.
13. Your child has increased stress and anxiety.
14. Your child may have a weakened immune system and up to a 500 percent increase in sicknesses.
15. Your child spreads disunity.
16. A closed heart may result in your child's own divorce later in life.
17. Your child may have a lower sense of self-value.
18. Your child usually has a victim mentality.
19. Premarital sex with pregnancy is a much greater possibility.
20. Angry outbursts and physical fighting may result.

The best commentary I have ever heard on Ephesians 6:1-4 was simply "Children obey your parents, and parents treat your children in a way that they want to obey." This study on memorizing and meditating will not work in a home where parents are provoking their children to anger and forcing them to memorize God's Word. Learn the best loving ways to motivate them, model it for them, create a hunger for it, and bring their heroes to your home with the same message of memorizing the Bible and meditating on it.

Parent Point

Help your child picture what his or her life will look like as a result of memorizing God's Word.

Parent Plan

One Final Caution: Never Force Your Children to Join You

Kids are kids. They are not as mature as some adults, and at young ages they have little or no interest in Scripture memorization. Naturally, you would like to change that. You want them to become interested in the Scriptures. You want them to hide certain basic passages in their hearts to give them beliefs that will guide their decisions and actions for their entire life. And so, in your zeal to do your best for them, you decide to have your nine-year-old and eleven-year-old memorize a short list of pertinent Scriptures. You drill them every night and insist that they meet certain memorization goals you set for them. And you are diligent in modeling the principle to them, memorizing Scripture right along with them.

But soon you may see that it's not working. Clearly they hate the memorization sessions. They dread the evening when they must meet with you and go through another round of memorization drudgery. The verses are not sticking in their minds, and their hearts are not into the process. What should you do? You dearly want them to have deep-seated, godly beliefs in their hearts. Should you force them to continue, saying, "This is for your own good, and though you hate it now, you'll thank me for it someday"?

No. If you force your kids to memorize against their will, criticizing them for their lack of interest in spiritual things and disciplining them for their attitude, you may achieve the opposite of what you want. You may close your children's hearts to you and, worse, close them to God through their anger. They will feel that you are overly controlling. If they sense any unloving condemnation or criticism from you, they will feel unsafe and insecure. Their hearts will be wounded, resentment can set in, and they may reject the values you are trying to instill into their lives. Anger is a real killer of a child's heart toward you and God. You can't allow anger to come between you and your children.

Remain diligent and alert to any signs of anger creeping into your child's heart. Humble yourself and admit to your children that you don't have a child-raising guidebook within you naturally. Ask them if they would help you bring them up as mature and healthy adults. They know a lot more than you think about how they would like to be treated by you. Just ask them, and try to pump them for additional information to expand your understanding of how to love them in the best ways for them.

The truly effective way to instill beliefs and values in your kids is through relationship. God created us for relationship: first, for relationship with Him, and second, for relationship with one another. The first time it's recorded that God ever called anything "not good" was before He created Eve. He saw that "it is not good for the man to be alone" (Genesis 2:18). Human beings need relationship. Because we are created for relationship, we long to feel safe, secure, and loved in the presence of another person. When we are in good relationships, love opens the heart to the other person. When the heart is open and love flows, then beliefs and values easily float along the stream of love, passing from one heart to another. When the relationship between parent and child is right, this transfer of beliefs and values happens naturally, with love as the catalyst.

Be attentive and you can find ways to interest your kids in Scripture. You might want to check out the organization called Awana Club International, which now exists in thousands of churches. It was created to help kids memorize at least one thousand Bible verses by the time they finish high school. And most of those awesome verses will fit within the four Red Beliefs. Awana helps your children meditate by reviewing the verses that they memorize. One speaker I heard talking about the Awana Club said that the research done by Awana's own organization has found that 50 percent of kids who memorize the Scriptures Awana suggests will most likely seek a vocation in some type of full-time ministry. And about 70 percent of Awana kids stay in the church after they graduate from college.

You can make the "Deuteronomy 6 thing" work in your family's life. When you love your children enough to maintain a continuing relationship with them, and when you develop real enthusiasm for God, your kids are sure to catch your fired-up attitude. And when they see you memorizing Scripture and making its principles work in your life, they may be inspired to join you in the process.

You might even try a little reverse psychology. Tell your kids that you have been wondering if they are old enough to start memorizing. It's an exercise for kids who are, well, exceptionally smart children. You may have to wait a little longer before they are ready. Before they are ready they will have to take a test, which you will give them at the proper time. Of course, they will insist that they take the test now. Give them three or four questions, not too simple, yet simple enough that you know for sure that they can answer at least three of them. Then when they pass the test, admit that they are indeed ready and give each a verse to memorize.

The point here is to avoid dragging your children into memorizing Scripture against their will. You don't want them to think of it as an unpleasant drudgery. Let them see the importance of it by the changes in your own life, your own enthusiasm for God and His words, your overwhelming love for them, and your obvious interest in their ultimate welfare.

Memorize and Meditate

Now faith is being sure of what we hope for and certain of what we do not see. . . . And without faith it is impossible to please God, because anyone who comes to him must believe that he exists and that he rewards those who earnestly seek him. (Hebrews 11:1,6)

Above all else, guard your heart, for it is the wellspring of life. (Proverbs 4:23)

That if you confess with your mouth, "Jesus is Lord," and believe in your heart that God raised him from the dead, you will be saved. For it is with your heart that you believe and are justified, and it is with your mouth that you confess and are saved. (Romans 10:9-10)

What comes out of a man is what makes him "unclean." For from within, out of men's hearts, come evil thoughts, sexual immorality, theft, murder, adultery, greed, malice, deceit, lewdness, envy, slander, arrogance and folly. All these evils come from inside and make a man "unclean." (Mark 7:20-23)

Do not be deceived: God cannot be mocked. A man reaps what he sows. The one who sows to please his sinful nature, from that nature will reap destruction; the one who sows to please the Spirit, from the Spirit will reap eternal life. (Galatians 6:7-8)

Verses for Guarding Your Heart

The Four Key Beliefs

God's Holy Spirit and His powerful words are released within my heart, building His godly beliefs so that I will reflect Him in my thoughts, words, actions, and emotions.

1. Humble Yourself

2 Chronicles 7:14

Psalm 1:1-6

Micah 6:8

Luke 6:45

Luke 9:23-25

John 1:12

John 3:16

John 17:17

Acts 1:8

Galatians 2:20

Galatians 6:7-8

Ephesians 2:8-9

Ephesians 4:26-27

James 4:6

1 John 1:9

2. Love God

Exodus 20:1-17
Deuteronomy 6:4-9
Psalm 139:17-18
Matthew 6:9-13
Matthew 22:36-40
John 1:1-2
John 1:14
John 5:24
John 6:63
John 8:31-32
John 14:23-26
Romans 6:23
Hebrews 11:1,6

3. Love Others

Matthew 5:23-24
Matthew 5:43-45
Matthew 7:12
Romans 12:10
1 Corinthians 13:4-8
Galatians 5:13-14
Philippians 2:2-8
James 1:19-20
1 John 3:16,18-20
1 John 4:7-8
1 John 4:19-21

4. Rejoice in Trials

Romans 5:3-5
Romans 8:28
2 Corinthians 10:4-5
2 Corinthians 12:9-10
Philippians 4:6-9
Philippians 4:19
1 Thessalonians 5:16-18
James 1:2-4

Verses Fitting All Four Beliefs

Psalm 119:9-11
Proverbs 4:23
Matthew 5:3-12
Matthew 6:33
Mark 7:20
Mark 12:29-31
John 15:4
John 16:7-16
Romans 10:9-10
Romans 12:2
Ephesians 3:16-20
Ephesians 6:1-4
Ephesians 6:10-13
Philippians 4:13
Colossians 3:1-17

Notes

1. Dr. Caroline Leaf, *Who Switched Off My Brain?* (Nashville: Thomas Nelson, 2009).
2. Dr. Caroline Leaf, *The Gift in You* (Nashville: Thomas Nelson, 2009), 171.

SESSION 1: Do You Have a Plan?
1. *The 9/11 Commission Report*, 13, http://www.9-11commission.gov/report/911Report.pdf.

SESSION 5: Practicing Humility in the Family
1. John Piper, "Six Aspects of Humility," http://www.desiringgod.org/Blog/1126_6_aspects_of_humility.

SESSION 6: Belief #2 — Love God
1. Here are two websites that explain who God is and what He does for us: http://www.sundayschoolresources.com/bdqualitiesofgod.htm and http://www.seekgod.org/bible/godis.html.

SESSION 8: Belief #3 — Love Others
1. C. S. Lewis, *Mere Christianity* (New York: HarperCollins, 1952, 2001), 131.

SESSION 9: Applying Our Love for Others
1. Dean Ornish, MD, *Love and Survival* (New York: HarperCollins, 1998).
2. Dr. Caroline Leaf, *The Gift in You* (Nashville: Thomas Nelson, 2009).

About the Author

DR. GARY SMALLEY is one of the country's best-known authors and speakers on family relationships. His books combined have sold more than six million copies. Many of them have been translated into various languages. *The Blessing* and *The Two Sides of Love* have won the Gold Medallion Award for excellence in literature. *The Language of Love* won the Angel Award as the best contribution to family life. All other titles have been top-five finalists for the Gold Medallion Award.

In the last forty years, Dr. Smalley has spoken to more than two million people in live conferences. He has been presenting his live two-day workshop "Love Is a Decision" once a month for the last twenty years. Television audiences all over the world have viewed his award-winning infomercial "Hidden Keys to Loving Relationships." Several versions of the infomercial—first with Dick Clark, then with John Tesh and Connie Sellecca, and also with Frank and Kathie Lee Gifford—have aired. This eighteen-videotape series has sold more than four million copies.

Dr. Smalley has appeared on national television programs such as *Oprah, Larry King Live, Extra, TODAY,* and *Sally Jessy Raphael* as well as numerous national radio programs. He has been featured on hundreds of regional and local television and radio programs across the United States.

Dr. Smalley and his wife, Norma, have been married for forty-five years and live in Branson, Missouri. They have three children (Kari, Greg, and Michael) and ten grandchildren.

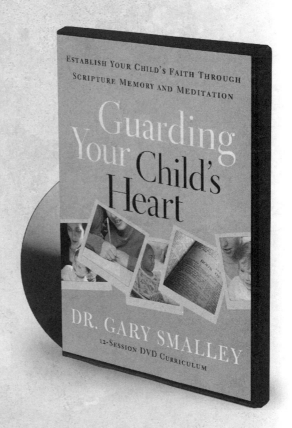

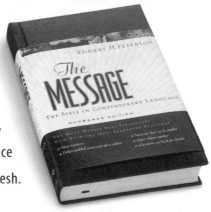